CW00376376

On Sacred Mountains

On Sacred Mountains

Martin J. Goodman

Heart of Albion

On Sacred Mountains
Martin J. Goodman

Cover illustration by Norman Fahy

ISBN 1 872883 58 3

Heart of Albion Press
2 Cross Hill Close, Wymeswold
Loughborough, LE12 6UJ

albion@indigogroup.co.uk

Visit our Web site: www.indigogroup.co.uk/albion/

Printed in the UK by Booksprint

For Robert Ott and Colleen Kelley
and also, of course, for James

Such narrow, narrow confines we live in. Every so often, one of us primates escapes these dimensions, as Martin Goodman did. All we can do is rattle the bars and look after him as he runs into the hills. We wait for his letters home
The Los Angeles Times

Martin Goodman is a mystic, poet and superb storyteller.
John Horgan, bestselling author of *The End of Science*

Heralds a new dawn for British writing.
Daily Post

Martin Goodman continues his hard-nosed approach to spiritual phenomena. He doesn't discount them; he tests them with his life! After his internationally acclaimed books *I Was Carlos Castaneda* and *In Search of the Divine Mother*, astonishing perspectives on the psychedelic shamanism of the Amazon and the guru / devotee relationship, comes this most powerful and daring of adventures.

What is a sacred mountain? Study them all we like, the only way of knowing them is to measure their effects in our own lives. Starting at Mount Ararat, moving to Ireland, passing through the sacred heights of India and Sri Lanka, Martin was then called to the mountain ranges of the American South West. At the highest point of Texas he received a revelation of great promise for the survival of humanity. His journey is a compelling story of intimate encounters, sexual transformation, astounding landscapes, and raw mountain energy. The writing is of a rare quality that turns each experience into our own.

Tune your life to higher powers – read this book and hear the mountains speak.

Martin Goodman shares his life between his
native England and mountain homes in
New Mexico and the south of France.

Please visit his website: www.MartinGoodman.com

Previously published books by Martin Goodman:

On Bended Knees
In Search of the Divine Mother
I Was Carlos Castaneda

Contents

1
Ararat
Eastern Turkey

"What will you do if I leave you?" the young woman sat up in bed and asked. We were living in Scotland. She was a mountaineer. I guess she had some other peak to climb.

"Sell my home and everything I own and set off on a journey around the world's sacred mountains," I replied. "Not like you, not as a mountain climber, I wouldn't want to conquer them."

"Ha ha ha!"

I got the subtext of her laugh. She doubted I would ever conquer anything.

"Each mountain is looked after by some sacred tradition. I'd work out the best way of approaching the place, and that's how I would go," I persisted. "It would be like a test. If these mountains are really powerful, and I approach them in the right way, I'd be changed. They'd make me better somehow."

Lorna laughed again.

I think she would have left me in any case.

A soldier slept on my shoulder. His was the boniest, heaviest head I had ever known. I didn't wake him. A boy spread a sheet of cardboard on the floor and slept at my feet. Our bus had started out from Istanbul, crossed the Bosphorus into Asia, and sped on through one of the more absurdly large countries in the world. Turkey is still an empire. It reaches west into Greece and Europe, but also stretches east till it's beyond the scope of the European mind. Just over its eastern mountains are Iran, Armenia, Georgia, Iraq and Syria. This is an Asia of fierce winters and fierce summers.

The soldier and the boy woke at dawn. The volcano of Tatvan across to our left erupted eons ago and sealed the exit to a sea. This sea is now Lake Van. Snowmelt fills it, and sun blasts down to shimmer its waters back to the skies. As we looked out at the volcano two foreigners were being kidnapped from its slopes. The news would make world headlines the following week.

Many climbed from our bus and took a minibus connection into town. The following month this same mini bus would be blown up and all those in it killed.

Our bus continued on the road around the lake, mountains now rearing to our right.

The following week a bus on this route would be stopped, and more foreigners hauled from it into mountain captivity.

I thought my own journey was a rough one, but then I wasn't reading the newspapers. In fact I was being treated kindly. The whole region was in ferment. My pilgrimage had brought me to a war zone.

The city of Van is modern. It is built a little inland from the water, closer to the mountains than its predecessor. The previous city was razed to the ground when Ottoman forces massacred its Armenian population in 1915. Estimates of the number of Armenians who lost their lives in this massacre vary between 50,000 and 500,000, the exact number a point of contention as much as sorrow. A certain fact is that many thousands perished on a forced winter march to Syria. A highlight of the local museum is a showcase filled with human remains, grey skeletons from the start of the twentieth century.

On my very first morning in Van I decided to take a break and leave the city behind me.

A pleasant group of young men shared the mini bus. They wanted to know what I did for a living.

"I'm a writer," I said.

"Ha!" they said. "Salman Rushdie!"

One man slit a finger across his throat, and the whole bus laughed. Apart from me. They decided I was their friend in any case.

Our ferryboat chugged out from the easternmost shore to part the waters of Lake Van. In twenty minutes we were bobbing by the landing stage of the holy island of Akdamar.

Kurdish men come and play here every Sunday afternoon in

summer. They link arms around each other's shoulders and dance on the island's shores. The music they dance to is banned in their towns and villages for it is Kurdish. The Turkish government seeks to suppress the Kurdish language and culture. Out here their dance is a chorusline of knee-bending struts, and they laugh to the notes of their songs.

An Armenian cathedral church, built between 915 and 921, stands to the side of the steps up from the sea. It is abandoned rather than ruined, its doors gone but its conical roof still layered in tiles. A few monks lived in the monastery buildings until the 1890's.

Frescoes faded on the interior walls and the floor was swept with dirt. My new friends hung around at my side, their bathing towels bright across their shoulders, and kicked up the dust. I freed them from etiquette, and said if they wanted to go and swim now I would join them later. They grinned and ran away.

The church seemed empty without them. A church was a church, I thought, and went outside.

Then I saw the wonder of it. The logic of this church had been inverted. The building was designed to be inside out, so that its joys are paraded along its outer walls. From the ground up to the roof honey-coloured stone carries sculptures peeled from the pages of some giant's illustrated bible. The Goliath in bas-relief truly is the size of a giant, with a cow curled in sleep by his ankles. A medallion of Christ looks out from above David's elbow as the barefoot boy lifts his sling. Adam and Eve meet the serpent curled around the tree, Jonah rides the whale in his sailing ship, Abraham tugs Isaac by his hair, while smaller figures of saints stroll the walls like fellow tourists in this Old Testament landscape. Some birds and beasts are sideways on, eyes looking straight ahead as they follow each other in a parade around the walls, but the main characters look out from the building, as people do when they're talking to you.

I love those images, so bold and so simple and right. Those biblical characters have been brought outside to stare full-time at the surrounding mountains. They are a happy expression of faith.

Akdamar Island is shaped like Gibraltar or a blunt-nosed whale, low at one end and high at the other. The route that led to its broad tip was steep. My sandals slid up a dusty track and I clambered over large white boulders till I reached the point where the land stops and a high cliff drops down to the sea.

I chose a boulder to be my throne and sat up above the world. The summer tops of the surrounding mountains were veined with grey ice. Seagulls, alpine swifts and kestrels spun their flights below me, cutting in as though to smash their bodies against the cliff's white walls then banking high with inches spare to shoot toward the sky.

Here I sat, proud and alone.

And a little lonely.

There is a grove on the ridge of the island above the church, its trees gathered around a patch of yellow grass. A dragonfly nestled on a twig, its thin body bright with a blue like compacted sky. The tip of its tail was joined to another dragonfly, stuck to a point behind its neck. This second creature kept its body inert as it was hoisted up and down by the other's tail.

They were mating.

It kept them occupied long enough for me to admire their colour, then I walked on down to the shore.

My friends were waiting.

Sunlight rippled over the wet muscles in a young man's back as he stood and looked across the water. He was twenty-one, a year or so older than the others. They showed me a photograph of him during his military service. He was scaling a mountain face on exercise, his body stretched and tensed against the rock. Freed from the army, he now stood facing the mountains that ring the water. Trained to fight, he was ready to do battle against the Turkish army who trained him. He would fight for his homeland, for Kurdistan.

I enjoyed the beauty of his back. The front of a body is divided into segments, but a back is purely a back. It is vulnerable and smooth. Muscles are subtle but alive. They play across a back as waves play across a sea. I could watch a back as beautiful as his for hours. It is one of the happiest meditations I can think of.

I slid down my rock and slipped away into the expanse of water.

Salt trapped in this inland sea has turned alkaline and gives the water the smoothness of soap. It buoyed me up as I turned the promontory into an inlet, then swam further to reach the cliff where the seabirds spiralled and swooped. Above me was the rock where I had been sitting. Birds swelled from specks to missiles as they dive-bombed the water around my head.

My new friends were puzzled by my vanishing, but waited for my return. They played a joke by looking in the wrong direction, pretending I had swum the full circuit of the island because I had been gone so long. They helped me from the water and fed me slices of watermelon along with a moist, herb-flavoured cheese.

It was food with the juice of medicine. Such kindness works the gradual cure of solitude.

A different group of young men filled the bus for my return to town. They greeted me with laughter and cries of recognition. It was the staff from my hotel. The hotel was new, and tourism so out of fashion in this dangerous time that I was their only guest. When I went out for the day, their hotel was empty so they followed me.

Back in the hotel restaurant they brought me a kitten for company. Cats from Van are famous in the world of cats, fluffy and white with mismatched eyes, one yellow and the other blue. This kitten came to me wrapped in a towel, and the towel was wet with its urine. I let the towel drop and held on to the animal.

Its mass of fur made up most of its weight, soft within my hands. The rest of the creature was ferocious. Its body squirmed and it slashed out with all its claws. I held on for a moment then let it drop. It darted off between the forest of furniture legs, escaping to the far corner of the room.

Some solitudes are spunky that way.

A slither of wall traces the top of the rock-mountain that used to dominate the old city of Van. A wrought-iron silhouette of Atatürk, the founding father of modern Turkey, crowns the summit. Towers and walls built from mammoth blocks of stone crumble around it, relics from three thousand years ago when this rock was the base of the Kingdom of Urartu.

Two mosques are left on the land between the rock and the lake, and a lone chimney stack. Narrow paths are threaded between humps of earth. The Rock of Van is the tombstone, and this the vast burial ground of the old city.

The Kurds trace their ancestry straight back to Noah, who is buried in the region. Noah of course knew a time when all the Earth's cities were swept from existence. That pattern of destruction lives on in the region. Survivors retreat to the mountains and so keep history alive.

I walked above the humps of the vanished city till the land grew flat once more. Lines of men were scything the acres of grass and loading it into horse-drawn carts. In the streams and rivers that cut through the ground young boys splashed golden and naked, leaping forward to grasp at fish with their bare hands.

Two boys, freshly dressed and ready to carry away their catch, gasped with surprise at the sight of me. Few foreigners wandered across their fishing ground. Then they recovered and laughed at themselves. Frogs shot through the air to plop in distant mud as I stepped down the stones of the bank to admire the boys' display of fish. They held up the small silver bodies one by one, then shrieked and jumped back. A snake had dropped down the far bank. It relaxed its body in the thin stream and floated away.

I turned back through a copse of planted trees to climb the Rock of Van. I make no great claims for this rock as a sacred mountain, and would not mention it but for my descent along a dusty path that angled down beneath the walls of the fortress. As I walked, a cloud of frail yellow butterflies floated with me. Scores of them flitted close by my sides as I trod through the midday heat, their wings whispering up a breeze.

There is public transport to most places in Turkey. You just have to find the right place by the roadside, wait for others to gather around you, and hope an appropriate *dolmus* (a minibus running as a shared taxi) will come along.

An old couple in the headgear of their faith, the lady shawled in blankets and the man sporting a lace skull-cap, planted themselves beside the driver on the front bench seat. Their bags of produce, as large and round as themselves, were stacked around my legs. The rest of us on board were young men, settling in for the 185 kilometre north-east route between Van and the town of Dogubayazit.

Noah's approach in his Ark was something like this. Our table of land was green and high and flat like some seas, with lines of lava waves cresting to either side. The waves were black, relics of some distant upheaval, square chunks breaking off their curling peaks to fall as fossilized foam. The source of this sea of lava, a black volcano capped with snow, stood above the plateau's horizon over to our left.

I considered that volcano. It was fine and mighty, but it fitted into the scope of my imagination. That would not do. It could not be Ararat. Ararat had to surpass all that I could imagine, or the huge overland journey to haul my body this far was a total waste of effort.

So where was this great mountain? Already our bus had tipped itself over the edge of the plateau to follow the road down to the plain. I could see our destination, the town of Dogubayazit, far below us to the right. The only mountains in view were a slender range of red ones, fine in themselves but diminutive.

My focus was narrowed to the earth, expecting a clear outline to rise from the plain.

I could not see for looking.

Ararat was there all along, a presence that filled the sky. The red mountain range was the lower rim of a broken frame, while Ararat was the painting. The sky to its sides and up above was blue and clear, while the peak was lost in billows of white cloud especial to itself. From those clouds spread the streaks of the mountain's snows, and it was these snows that gave the mountain its form. Below the snowline the mountain was dark and simply a shadow, but the white of the snow caught the light of the day and reflected it as brilliance.

Reason explained that the mountain thrust itself up out of the earth, but the vision told of something that streamed down from the skies as we watched.

Dogubayazit is a frontier town. The *dolmus* drivers here ask to ferry you on the short hop to Iran. The buildings to either side of the main street are unimaginative squares of cinder block. A little wealth is pumped in through cross-border traffic and tourism, and so another tier is added to the buildings. The trade pauses for a while, and so the buildings in progress stop as they are.

My hotel, the Ishfahan, was notionally the best in town. It used to be popular with trekking groups for Ararat and parties determined to find Noah's Ark, but for now I was the only guest. Times had been better. The military had placed Ararat firmly out of bounds, so that anyone walking there was asking to be shot.

I stroked a finger along the hotel walls and it came away black. No lights worked along the corridors and the restaurant was shut. Standards seemed to be slipping. I stumbled through the dark to find my room, then reported back to the desk clerk.

"The room will do," I explained. "But the hotel is filthy. And why are there no lights?"

I should consider myself lucky, the desk clerk explained. Two days ago the hotel was gutted by a firebomb attack. It was good for me that they were open at all. Every day I was there the hotel would become cleaner and better, and its facilities would work a little more.

"Is it safe now?" I asked.

"Oh yes. After dark you must stay inside. In your room. Then you are safe."

I could not complain, since I had come at my own risk. In Istanbul an official from the British Consulate had warned me against travelling East. News was coming back through their information network saying that foreigners and hotels were to be targetted by the PKK. The PKK is the Kurdish Workers' Party, a group waging guerilla warfare against the national armed forces. They were fighting for a separatist state in eastern Turkey. I learned later that the firebomb attack on my hotel was by a group from the PKK. The hotel's owner had just been up to one of the PKK base camps in Iran. His son was fighting with the group but the owner dragged him home. In reprisal the group had set fire to his hotel.

The whole region was pulsing with hostile acts of one kind or another. Just as I arrived in the city of Van a hotel was being burned to the ground. The hotel was home to some Russian women who had been brought across the border to work as prostitutes. The attack was by Islamic fundamentalists on religious grounds. Tourists died alongside the ladies.

A man in Dogubayazit told me of his cousin who had been seen walking on the streets with a Russian woman just the week before. He had been shot dead.

"It's OK," he explained as I tried to commiserate. "Families are very big here. We have hundreds of cousins."

I thanked the desk clerk for his information and went back up to my room. When Dogubayazit starts buzzing again, when war ebbs and trading resumes, builders will return to the worksite opposite my hotel and the view from my balcony will be lost. For the present I was content to sit a while and admire the spread of Ararat above the rooftops.

Just a few steps beyond the main road to and from the Iranian border, lanes are squeezed between high walls of mud. I walked through them. The sun-baked walls of homes revealed nothing of themselves but their children. At every intersection, at every gateway, more of them ran in to trot along with the pack.

"Pul," they shouted, a demand for money. "Pul. Pul. Pul. Pul." They stamped up dust in the rhythm of their chant, and slapped their hands about my trouser pockets that were sealed with an armoury of zips.

As the crowd of children grew loud a man appeared, his flat-capped head leaning through a gateway. He shouted a command that scattered the kids and cleared the lanes before he himself withdrew.

Another man stepped out to greet me. Some men of this region are giants. This one was small, smaller than me, but otherwise typical. He wore the traditional cloth cap and dark suit, his shirt was buttoned to the collar, and a thick moustache grew above his gap-toothed smile. He spoke some German and wanted to tell me about the mountain.

He was a shepherd, he said, but a sorry one. He used to graze his flock on the mountain pastures. The journey up would take him two days. He climbed as high as two thousand metres but no further, for beyond that it was too cold to sleep. Then he would take two more days to come down. That was the pattern of his life until three years ago, when the mountain was put out of bounds. It was patrolled now by the military and forbidden to him and his herds.

He held out his hand toward a curly-haired boy in the ring of youngsters that surrounded us. This was his relative. Shepherding skills of the slopes of Ararat had been handed down through the generations, but now they were destined to fade away. He would die and the sum of his shepherding skills would die with him.

Confined to those lanes, children learned what skills they could. I whirled around as a hand reached in for the contents of my backpack. The kids backed off a little, but not far. Another man appeared in the lane, a larger man. He barked a command. The kids scattered. I took my chance and hurried out of the warren of lanes to the broader streets of the town.

I hoped to climb the forbidden mountain a little before being turned back. The plain I had to cross was already at a height of 1800 metres. Sparse grass grew on top of cracked mud as I strode through the first hour of my hike. Then the colour of the grass changed, from brown through yellow to green. It grew thicker and reached up to my ankles, thicker still to cover my thighs, kept on growing to hide my chest, and then collapsed into the waters of a wide stream.

The waters running off this mountain are such that the Arabs considered Ararat to be the roof of the world. It was from here that two great rivers, the Tigris and Euphrates, were thought to have their source. I was faced with retreating from my quest, pushing my way back through the grasslands, or testing the waters.

Bubbles sprang from my first footstep in the mud, small brown frogs that skittered to all sides. Wings cracked and a duck shot up in vertical flight. Bulrushes pierced the sky above my head as I sank in water to my knees. Sheep must feel as confused as this, pushing their way through a dip. It was appropriate, I supposed, since Ararat was the first of my sacred mountains. I was being baptized, cleansed, purified, and soaked, before setting foot on its slopes.

The grass on the far side of the waters was luscious and soft. Beyond it was a drystone wall. I climbed it and dropped down to the other side. This was it. It would take several more miles of ascent to bring me to the summit, but I was already on Ararat. Arms out to my side I ran uphill, cresting the outermost wave of a lava flow, excited to see what lay beyond.

What lay beyond was the dogpack from hell. Imagine Irish wolfhounds that have swallowed their wolf, their coats thick tangles of hair, their fangs snapping shut on the roars of their barking, then shaking the slather off their gums as they ripped the sounds apart; this was my welcoming dogpack. They wore collars of spikes. Five of them choreographed their approach. They had no need to leap. They could have just turned their heads to one side and snapped out my throat. Instead they let me run. A new drystone wall bordered a farmstead. I reached its open gate and ran inside.

No dog followed.

To them I was a sheep. They were sheepdogs. I had come through the sheepdip and now they had rounded me up. The farmstead was my pen and I was safe inside.

A man was bent over a cart in a corner of the farmyard, surrounded by children. They tugged his sleeve and turned him round. He walked toward me. I took his hand when he held it out. His eyes were open but he looked to the side of my head rather than at my face. He was blind. The children chattered around him so that he heard what they saw, and he invited me into his home.

Its roof was made of earth, its ceiling of straw. The stones of the walls were rounded like gingerbread, and snuggled together. The walls inside were plastered, their brightest decoration two blue nylon backpacks hanging side by side from nails. The floor was carpeted green, the green that emerges with excitement from under the snows of winter. Cushions were set like a sofa opposite the open door.

I settled down and said yes to tea. A child ran off with the news. Sticks were collected in some other part of the house, a fire was laid, water gathered for the pot, and sugar chopped for the bowl. Teatime came later in the rhythm of their day, but they had inverted their routine for my sake.

Conversation was hard. We shared no language, and while I like to speak with my hands these could not be seen by the blind man. I barked and growled like dogs and my host understood. His own hands were expressive. They clamped themselves about his throat, then he pulled them away to trace a finger along the puckered line of a scar.

Yes, the dogs round here could be dangerous, he was telling me. It was an attack by dogs like those outside his walls that had rendered him blind.

We spoke of our countries, of his blindness, and we listed the cities that would belong to the new Kurdistan. He taught me my first words of Kurdish, which I applied as the gracious pattern of his hospitality unfolded.

"*Hodishterrazibbie*," I said, my version of a Kurdish thank you, as glass after glass of tea was poured from white enamel pots splashed with large orange flowers.

"*Zaverunde*," meaning wonderful, as I praised a vast platter of hot pitta breads, each the size of a coffee table, that came alongside a bowl of goat's cheese and another of yogurt.

The children, a brood of about a dozen, peered in round either side of the doorway. The baby of the troupe, a small girl with raggled fair hair, took hold of my discarded boots and marched them across the top step. When she tired and cried a brother carried her in and nestled her for instant comfort in her father's arms. A blue glass eye, a lucky charm, was tied by a string to the short sleeve of her pullover. Her own eyes ran, her nose streamed. I pressed a tissue into the father's hand, guided it up to the nose he could not see, and he dabbed his daughter's face dry.

The dogs were gone as I carried on my way up the mountain. Two women came running from a small hut-like house of stone and stood alongside the path. Word had got through of the new man in town.

They were decked out in national costume, a startling assortment of primary colours, embroidery filling their aprons and hats. They still held their mirrors, for they had added the final touches to their beauty while standing by the path. They blushed eagerly through their makeup, a fusion of colours like a sunset meeting a moon, and their smiles were emboldened with deep red lipstick. Their teeth had many gaps to slide a tongue between.

They lifted their arms to invite me back to their hut. Their arms jangled with bangles. I thanked them but moved on. They giggled and watched me leave.

A track led uphill from the village. I took my first steps along it, and was stoned.

The stones were small ones and flung by youngsters. The ones that hit me would barely bring up bruises. The boys lined the path behind me as their arms flailed with their throws. Their young voices burst with insults. A man stepped out of the nearest farmyard to call them off, then returned to his work.

The old are hospitable, but the young have learned new ways. In one of the widest landscapes on earth they have been cramped by civil war. Whole villages have been razed for giving hospitality to one side or another. Foreign agents with skin like mine were seen as provoking the whole conflict.

The kids chucked stones. They have learned that hospitality can leave a curse on those who provide it.

The trail rose through a dwarfing landscape. I was squeezed into insignificance by outcrops of black lava many times my height. The volcano had flowed this way. It was no place for human beings.

Locals tell a tale of the twin peaks of Agri Dag, the local name for Ararat. I could see them before me now. Little Ararat at 13,055 feet was a small dark cone across to my right. At 17,112 feet and straight ahead, Great Ararat was somewhat taller than her sister. The sisters once quarrelled, the local story said. Hot-tempered as only volcanoes can be, they wished a curse upon each other.

Great Ararat had experienced all the creatures of the earth trotting from the Ark and down her sides. Having found the experience less than good, she wished a plague of animals and snakes upon her sister. The creatures are there still. Before the current troubles Little Ararat was a favoured place for huntsmen, where they could pick off creatures two by two.

Meanwhile Little Ararat dealt with her envy of her sister's size. Great Ararat had eternal snows wished upon her to blank out her upper half. This snow appears to the onlooker as a vision, snow as a bright and floating cap that crowns the earth and hangs from the heavens.

A streak of white cloud circled the summit as I watched, clockwise and around and around, so that for moments it was brilliantly clear before the cloud swirled back to veil it. This cloud seemed like proof that the mountain was not still but turning. Sticks gather candyfloss in the same way. This sacred mountain was turning as the axis of the world.

I sat and gazed the sight in like a flower that turns to the sun, with the instinct that it could do me good and help me grow. Then I cut an oblique path back down the slopes and toward the town, so as to arrive there before sunset and the curfew.

The roar of an engine smashed through the silence. I looked around but could see nowhere obvious to hide, and whatever the vehicle was it was coming too fast. I feared the army as I feared the guerilla units, for neither group would want to find me on this territory. A truck appeared and braked to a halt, dust spewing up around its wheels as men jumped down from the cab.

I was lucky. These were not armed units but workers ferrying rock down from the mountain's side. They invited me to jump on board. I found footholds on the large and brittle lava boulders of its load. Gripping the rail on top of the cab I flexed my legs. I was surfing. Surfing lava as it sped down Ararat's side.

The speed was thrilling. We roared into a warm wind and I angled my body to curve round corners. We squeezed between outcrops like they were hairpin bends on a racetrack, the truck's wheels bouncing off the earth then skimming back down again. Then the truck found a stretch of level ground and slowed to a halt.

We had come a long way in so short a run. I could see down to the main road, and the cloud of dust above the factory where our load of rock would be pummelled to gravel.

"Very fast," I said, and signalled the story of speed and bouncing rocks with my hand.

"No brakes," a man from the cab stood and called back. I understood his Kurdish from his mime. He signalled a useless brake pedal, and panic. The driver dived under the engine hood and started pulling at cables.

I carried a message they wrote in my notebook. It was a message to the PKK, the Kurdish guerrilla group, introducing me if I was stopped so that I would not be harmed. And the message was also the news that the Turkish government was slaughtering their kinfolk and clearing their villages, news which I must take with me and tell to my world.

"*Kurdistan zaverunde*," I shouted, to cheer them up, and punched the air.

I headed on, but turned to look at Ararat again before jumping down the final metres to the plain. The summit was hidden from sight by an escarpment of rock, but another treat stood in its place.

Ararat sends messages through birds. Noah received good news with the return of his dove and an olive leaf.

I, in my turn, was granted an eagle. It was dark against the sky, its wing tips feathered to catch the current of the breeze. It rode high, hovered for a while, then swooped low and out of sight. Its flight had mapped the shape of Ararat upon the air.

~~~~~~~~~~
~~~~~~~~~~

Trace any family tree of any animal back through time, and tradition teaches that we find ourselves on Noah's Ark. All of our journeys on earth can be said to have started on Mount Ararat. Its slopes gave us momentum.

When I first considered the nature of my journey around sacred mountains, I made one decision. The mountains had to be representatives of different cultures. If my journey worked it would become a book. If the book was to work, I didn't want readers to see the experiences as alien to themselves. A book on the sacred mountains of India, for example, could be dismissed as 'a Hindu thing'. I wanted to visit a wide enough range of mountains so that readers could begin to look for a sacred mountain close to home.

Ararat is one of the crowns of central Asia. Its slopes gave momentum to my journey. The month of July saw me streaking across the continents, bound for Europe's westernmost tip. Faster than a mountain goat released from Noah's Ark, I stepped from a superspeed ferry and on to Irish shores.

I had moved from one zone of civil war, to another.

2
Croagh Patrick
Ireland

Scores of thousands of pilgrims wait for the last Sunday of July each year to travel to the West Coast of Ireland. They drink and dance through Saturday night in the pubs of Westport, then join the mass ascent into the clouds that swathe the peak of Croagh Patrick. I set off to join them.

Belfast railway station greeted me with a rainstorm. I splashed off for a walk.

An armoured car was parked in the middle of the road and a soldier stood on the pavement. I passed him then looked back. His sight was trained along the barrel of his rifle, which pointed at my head.

It was genetic. He had smelled the Irish blood in me.

My mother's father was known as Pat O'Neill. He grew up in England, but that wasn't his fault. His father was a gypsy who worked the racecourses of Ireland as a profession. His mother gambled on love, and lost. Pat O'Neill was born, an illegitimate child, and his mother died of a broken heart. She broke the heart herself, it seems, once love had let her down.

My grandfather was brought up by relatives in Leicester. He slaved as a stoker, worked as an auxiliary policeman, and named his three daughters with the fine Irish names of Kathleen, Maureen and Bridget. Every story tells of his love and fairness. My grandmother hammered the keys of the piano at impromptu parties as Pat sang Irish ballads in a fine tenor voice. He never drank more than three halves of beer but was always the heart of a gathering. He was a myth of my childhood, a model to grow by.

He died when my mother was fifteen. The loss marked her life and so mine.

There was once a prime minister of Ireland called O'Neill. Never one to miss a good story when she could think one up, my mother assured me he was our relative. I felt sorry for him in the troubles of his political life, and pleased to be so connected.

This arrival in Belfast was no homecoming, but I am linked to the land through such family tales. And it was good to find a sacred mountain so close to home, with a story that forms the roots of Christian Ireland.

Pleasant hills in the south of Ulster run out long before Dublin, from where the country stays flat all the way across to the west coast. In this sparsely populated land passengers shunt themselves along the train to stand in the portion that matches the length of the station platform, where the trim grey stone railway buildings manage to hide any town that might lie behind them.

The last Sunday in July was approaching, the day of the annual pilgrimage up Croagh Patrick in County Mayo, and it was a typical day of summer. Torrents of rain fell between bursts of sunshine. The country was absurdly green. There were too few cattle and sheep to trim the grass in fields so tiny they were almost swallowed by their hedges. Cows waded through the deep tussocks and pasture, reaching up to nibble the choicest tips from stalks that grew above their heads.

Approaching the west coast the land rippled a little, the folds growing larger toward the sea, but it was still patchworked by hedges into fields. It is only near the town of Westport, from where the sea takes over to cover the many miles to America, that the land surges into the bolder shape of the mountains of Mayo.

The date for this annual Christian pilgrimage up Croagh Patrick has danced around the calendar, but in settling for the last Sunday in July has slotted back into a more ancient tradition. Worship on the mountain has been traced back five thousand years. The Pagan God Lugh gave his name to the Irish word for August, Lughnasa, and a festival in his honour was held on the mountain's slopes. Locals know the mountain as the Reek, and their festival day as Reek Sunday.

Modern pilgrims are conscious of climbing in the footsteps of Saint Patrick. This saint climbed to the summit in 441 to spend the forty days and nights of Lent in prayer and fasting. Black birds mocked him with their stabbing flights, to be cast by legend as flocks of demons. Patrick sent them flying from the mountain's heights and cleared the way for angels to drop down and minister to him, but with them he was no less steadfast. Three times they refused to grant his chosen wish, that Ireland should keep the Christian faith till the last coming, for they knew the horrors this fate would involve. On the fourth time of his asking they relented.

Saint Patrick stood with his bell (still to be seen in the National Museum of Ireland in Dublin) and flung it down a chasm known as Lugnagoul on the north-east side of the mountain. The angels caught the bell at the bottom and threw it back, again and again till the clamour of its ringing roused the demons and serpents to slither from existence into a hollow on the mountain's north side.

It is the story of the taming of the mountain. There is no denying the power of Croagh Patrick, with its winds and mists and rockfalls that can snatch a person's life. But pilgrims who climb within the spirit of a saint are in a gentler realm than the one that saint first breached.

I primed myself on the Saturday of the weekend pilgrimage with a low level walk out from Westport, taking a hill road from the statue of the Saint in the town square toward Clew Bay and its eighteenth century harbour buildings. The Bay is packed with grassy islets like stepping stones cast across the Atlantic, several promontories along the walk taking the sea from sight to return it as a fresh view, the black mass of Croagh Patrick capping the line of hills that forms the final spur to the bay.

It has the conical shape I was coming to recognize as belonging to sacred mountains, a triangle that in this Catholic country might be read as a symbol of the Trinity. It is made of Silurian quartzite rock, but it can look like a volcano. Standing 2,510 feet (765m.) high, its peak is generally sliced from view by grey cloud.

Beyond the bay a narrow hedged road led me into the hills, sleepwalking past a vital tourist-board sign that marked the established route. My new way took me down past a school football ground, its goal posts made from sticks still covered in bark. A boulder rose from the turf to fill one quarter of the pitch, the mountainside including itself in every game.

Below the school was the plain known as Owenwee Bog. It was a vast wilderness of peatland, a tawny stretch toward distant hills.

I marched along it. Torrents fell to drench me, the sun and wind teamed up to steam and whip me dry, as I followed the base of the ridge of hills that lead westwards. These billow in two large waves, coloured a golden brown to catch the moments of sunlight, as though the peatland had flung up its blanket of grass to camouflage the heights. There was no disguising the summit though, the conical head of this recumbent body of earth, dark and still brooding inside the gloom of its cloud. This was Croagh Patrick.

It was good to have walked so far. It seemed right to have approached the mountain on foot. And now I had my excuse to rent a bike for the following day.

"Bigger than Christmas, it was," a lady mused from her bar stool in Westport that night.

All the pubs were packed, youngsters running round picking up the empties. The lady's blue eyes swam in the soft focus of memories and drink. The shorter strands of her grey hair had come loose from their bands, and jigged a little to the reels from the folk musicians in the corner as she nodded her head just out of rhythm. She fingered the string of wooden beads around her neck, like it was a rosary, like this would give her balance.

"All through the night, these pubs were open. All through and into the next day. Then we'd pile out of here and into buses, climb to the summit, then hurry back to town and the pubs again. Lots went at night. Some came back, some didn't. They tipped over the edge in a stupor. They've banned that now, more's the pity. It was an adventure, that was. Still, you'll find yourself skipping over pools of vomit if you start dead early."

She turned to the bar, reached around for her refuelled glass of Guinness, and planted the white moustache of its foam on her upper lip. She licked it off. It fuelled another memory. In gratitude for the pint she told another story.

"Do you know the tale of Gertie? Crippled she was, couldn't walk a step without her zimmer. Her son comes for her, dear if simple, and off they trot. It's midnight when they start out from the base. Her son gets down on his knees in front of her, takes hold of her left leg, and moves it forward a step. Then he shifts backwards, takes hold of her right, and moves that too. Step by step they go, all the way to the top and all the way down again. It's eight o'clock the next evening before the pair of them are back at the base."

She sipped her drink, smacked her lips.

"She's dead now, poor old Gertie. They say she climbed to heaven. Wonder how long that took her.

"Did you hear too of the other young man, nobody's son that anyone knows of, who lives twenty miles from the Reek? Every year he leaves his shoes by his front door, walks barefoot all the way to the mountain's top, then all the way back home again. Lovely feet, he has. I've seen them. It's nice they come out to get admired once a year."

My rented bike had eighteen speeds. More than I had myself. Technically out of my league, I figured the best I could do was pedal and hope. I rode the bike up to the top of the first hill out of town, and something snapped. The pedals whirred with no resistance and the machine stopped. I coated my hands in oil and was bewildered.

St Patrick's first approach to the mountain was not simple either. He was speeding in a chariot when his charioteer died. The saint buried the man and carried on. I carried on too, scooting down the hills and pushing the bike up them.

I chanced upon a farmer on the other side of his gate. He claimed little expertise on the subject of bikes, but stepped over to give mine a look.

I am not a great one for mechanics. When my first car dropped its rotten exhaust pipe on the road I did not know such a mishap was possible. I reported its loss as theft to the local police. The policeman I spoke with was still laughing as I hung up the phone.

The farmer had my bike's problem diagnosed in a moment.

"Where's its chain?" he asked.

A couple of miles back, it seemed. I presumed the Irish had invented a chainless bike. He offered to store the bike in his yard till my return, and wheeled forward his own for me to borrow. It was a bike in miniature, with white wheels the size of dinner plates, a well-rusted red frame and three speeds. I felt instant friendship toward it, and promised to travel in style.

"You may and you may not," the farmer laughed, and waved me on.

For the final mile the road was lined with cars. Tired of the incline, I rested the bike against the cushion of a hedge and walked this last stretch.

Twenty years ago there were claimed to have been 100,000 attracted to the pilgrimage. This year Reek Sunday clashed with a Connacht Football Final, where 26,000 would watch Mayo playing Rossmana. I heard of locals who had managed to reach the summit early before setting off for the match, offering a quick prayer for a victory (it worked), but it seemed from the talk in the pub that most people were either going to one event or the other. Calculations after the day suggested 20,000 made it to the top, and to me who knew no better it seemed substantial enough.

There seemed to be no particular time to start the climb. As I began my own ascent at nine o'clock there were as many coming down as going up, and when I came down again at one it was as true the other way round.

A statue of Saint Patrick, old and bearded and robed, stands near the base of the mountain. Though not one of the official stations of the way, pilgrims use it to practice on, circling a few times before climbing higher. A Papal indulgence has been granted to any who climb the mountain on Saint Patrick's Day or in the summer months and pray for the Pope's intentions. Being no Catholic I made do without the indulgence, but prayed that the Pope had some good intentions nevertheless.

The first stretch of path washed our feet and boots. Stones made it firm underfoot, but the path carried water to become a shallow stream. Men stood to the side of a narrow gateway through which everyone had to pass, and handed out their religious tracts.

The path persisted, still wet but sometimes running as parallel narrow tracks to allow the up and down streams of folk. The view of the conical peak lay across to the right, the summit mostly obscured by cloud but occasionally cleared. Here too was my first sight of the continuous line of pilgrims, stretching up the hill then bearing right to begin the final trek, figures receding to distant specks.

The image came to mind that we humans were like corpuscles in the mountain's artery, a to-and-fro that carried its life-blood of devotion.

Round we went, seven times, a chain gang circling a pile of stones called Leacht Benain. It's the first "station", a ritual breathing place from the ascent. Owenwee Bog lay on the plain beneath us, its pattern of cut rectangular peat fields awash with rain and glistening in the sunlight.

The final haul is scree, mostly large chunks of rock but these were sometimes spattered in mud and the path occasionally reduced to earth. I was glad of my birch staff. Many of these were for sale at fifty pence a time at the start of the walk, and most people but me bought one. I was regretting my decision not to when a lady on her descent presented me with her own. I dug it into the ground to save myself from many a tumble.

Mountain rescue volunteers were lining what they considered the acceptable bounds of the route, calling back those who threatened to wander off and rebuking those who were racing without respect. Teams of youngsters in red outfits from the Order of Malta ambulance brigade were also on hand, stretchering down the few with split skulls and twisted ankles. I saw several fall down, and on these slopes it must have hurt, but no-one complained. Each person laughed the surprise out of their body and got up to walk on.

I knew I was near the top on hearing the public address system. A priest was intoning the opening to the mass, celebrated every half hour on Reek Sunday at the newly whitewashed chapel built up here in 1905. He stood in his vestments, white with a gold bib, in a glass extension tacked on to the chapel's front. His congregation gathered in a semi-circle outside, flanked by two long lines, one outside a side door labelled 'Confessions' and the other by the door to the right, headed 'Holy Communion'. These lines of pilgrims were processed through two wide corridors within the church to exit by its rear doors, while others walked their fifteen ritual circuits of the church or stood still with their lips silently fluttering a prayer.

Patrick drove out the demons but something of their breath remained in the wind. The summit was alive with a flurry of litter, potato chip packets whirling in sharp spirals of wind and drinks cans rattling fast across the rocks.

A marketplace was active on the mountain top, crisps and snacks and cups of hot soup being sold from two stalls set up with the addition of tarpaulin roofs in the ruins of old stone huts.

Donkeys still worked as pack animals to carry these goods. They were tethered in the shelter of other stone ruins on the mountain's side. I ate my sandwich in their company then moved across the wide expanse of rock to sit for a while on the seaward side.

I had hoped for the magnificent Atlantic view from a summit clear of clouds. The occasional swirl of wind ripped open a gap wide enough for me to see through to the shore below, but it was a very chill wind that more constantly blew vapours of cloud across my face. I had been granted the view granted to Patrick, who an early chronicle tells us 'could not see the face of the sky and land and sea'.

The congregation listened to a sermon - my first sermon on a mount. The priest advised each of us pilgrims not to think of ourselves as one of a crowd. Our passage up the mountainside, a mountain St Patrick baptized in the name of Christ, had brought us out of the normal run of life. It was an example of careful progress made with sights ever pitched on God.

I watched a woman lead her tiny daughter up the mountain path. The girl wore white sandals, and the flat black shoes of the mother had tops that were cut to barely cover the toes. It was adequate footwear for crossing a street to visit a neighbour. Maybe these were their only shoes, or maybe they had dressed up for the day. Some men had put on their Sunday best for the mass at the top, looking smart in jackets, collars and ties and with their stout shoes well polished. Most others had come in their walking gear, from tee-shirts to anoraks, with boots, trainers or wellington boots on their feet.

Some young men walked bare chested, their bodies white and muscled with long locks of dark hair reaching down to their shoulders. This was a gypsy tradition. Maybe these gypsies were my kin on my mother's side of the family.

And there were those who walked barefoot.

They weren't many. I saw about thirty amongst the thousands during my own walk. They walked singly or in pairs, with one group of three, a man and his two daughters, young women who looked as twins though they were born about a year apart, tall where their father was short, with long tresses of dark hair and long blue nylon anoraks, flanking the man who could not stop smiling he was so happy, all three pairs of feet stepping in unison.

Several of those barefoot pilgrims did in fact smile, and I saw none grimace with pain. They seemed pleased with their feet when they looked down, treading carefully. The skin was white, the tops of the feet splashed grey, and the soles brown with mud.

Before coming to this day I had doubted the wisdom of approaching a sacred hill in such a throng. I had this notion that it was better to come alone, to seek some silent mystical communion.

I was wrong. This was a great lesson from my mountain journey. There was no need to set myself apart.

Of the pilgrimage day I expected a singing, jigging, festive crowd, a carnival procession with massed choirs on top.

I found none of that.

Instead I met with a friendliness so that when I caught someone's eye we both smiled. Twin streams of people flowed around each other, one up and one down. Everybody seemed beautiful, the young and the old, the shabby and the smart. We were all making an effort. Without each one of us, the stream would have been less.

While climbing up I had passed a barrel of a man with a ragged grey beard and a big belly. '1000 MILE RIDE' was emblazoned in white across his black top with its ring round the collar. He was a priest, puffing with effort.

A bucket was waiting at the bottom in which people could throw their money for his cause. The priest was Father Butler of the Oblate order, 68 years old and fundraising for his mission to the street kids of Brazil. This walk up Croagh Patrick was the final stage of his round-Ireland sponsored cycle journey, that had started in Dublin to end at mass on the summit.

I dropped some money into the priest's bucket. We were fellow cyclists after all.

I pulled the farmer's toy bike out of its hedge, and pedalled so fast the Irish landscape blurred into a dream of my own childhood.

~~~~~~~~~~~
~~~~~~~~~~~

My route from Ararat through Croagh Patrick had me on a direct course to America. Those islets that crossed Clew Bay were like stepping stones across the Atlantic. The gods of Indian mountain stories would not have hesitated. A few quick strides across the bay and they would have leapt the final distance of the ocean.

I didn't know America was to be part of the journey, however. The mountain gods of India had to teach me a few lessons before I was ready for the place. As Catholics climb Croagh Patrick each July, Hindus were set to flock to Arunachala in November. This southern Indian mountain is revered by those in the know as the most sacred place on earth. Mount Kailas in Tibet is revered as the abode of the supreme god Shiva. Arunachala is seen as being Shiva himself, the supreme god incarnate.

It was the first sacred mountain I ever heard of. I had no idea at the time what could make a mountain sacred, but when I read its name in a book it never left me.

Arunachala. Arunachala.

It kept on calling.

Croagh Patrick was a dry run on familiar ground. Now it was time for one of the most unfamiliar patches of ground on the globe.

3
Arunachala
Tamil Nadu, India

It was 1896 and a seventeen-year old boy travelled by train to the Indian town of Tiruvannamalai. A mountain spanned the sky, and he headed directly for it. He walked through the dirt streets, through the paved courtyards of a great temple which had spread itself at the foot of the mountain, entered a dark building at the temple's heart, and moved on through that toward a grey stone shrine at its very centre. The walls of the shrine were tarred to black by the smoke from a perpetual flame. He passed this fire and stopped in front of a stone, large and black, shaped like a phallus and dressed in a bright costume of gold and silk.

The boy wrapped his arms around the stone and hugged it close to his body. He wept with relief. He had found the object of his love.

As a younger child he had swooned a lot. His friends played with his trance-filled body, passing it round above their heads. He loved to send his body on dangerous dives into the waters of rivers and wells too. It was his favourite sport. His body seemed to go on separate journeys in this way, while his consciousness set itself apart.

At sixteen he lay down in his family's house and experienced death, saw that though his body was dead he was still aware of the fact, and so recognized human existence was not tethered to the body.

The boy now released the stone, took off his clothes to go naked, and found a crypt where he sat for several weeks. Insects bit him, boys threw stones, and he was happy.

He was home.

The mountain had called him, and planted its name inside his young head. Arunachala. He had repeated the name till his body responded and brought him here. Arunachala. Arunachala. The mountain was his father, his Lord, and himself. The boy and the mountain would come to be seen as one.

He grew up. People came to sit with him, look at him, and so feel happy. He found other places to sit, other places to live, but he never left the mountain's side. His mother moved in with him, and when her legs could no longer cope with mountain gradients they all moved down to what is now his ashram nestling beside the mountain's base. He was a good son. When his mother died he declared her a fully enlightened being, and built a small temple in her honour.

His name was Ramana Maharshi. In 1950 his body died, but people still come to sit with him. They perceive him as one of the most holy beings of all time.

I came too.

Irish rain is simply the liquid condition of the sky. For rain with passion, southern India in November is the place to be.

The palm trees by the shore were pressed down by the monsoon, bowing in the direction of the sacred mountain of Arunachala a few hundred miles inland. The rains streamed in above the Indian Ocean, building up speed to rush across the miles and fall as close as possible to the mountain's slopes.

This is what weather does when it's blown near to the heart of the world.

I took a bus inland. My rucksack was on my lap, and my English hide-bound soul somewhere in tow, ready to be stripped. I was ready to be seared by my first sight of the mountain.

The bus was packed and yammering, splurging through the mud and blaring its two-tone horn. The bus station of Villapuram was cratered with muddy pools. I swapped buses and won gentler progress, along a straight and narrow asphalt road through fields flush with green shoots of rice. It was like an approach to a British stately home in summer, lined with sturdy green trees and people dressed for brightness.

I saw the south gopuram first, one of nine mighty towers that career skywards from the temple complex of Tiruvannamalai. The temple was laid out in worship at the foot of Arunachala. The town gathered its low buildings to either side of the road. I saw the temple, but I could see no mountain.

I should have known better. I had lived among mountains in Scotland, where I sat at my desk and knew fear as cloud bulked over a clear mountain summit and heaped itself down like an avalanche. I had been on the side of Croagh Patrick and had it snatched away from view. This was the normal form of those Celtic mountains, this merging of mists and land and cloud.

My mountain was up there all along, outlined as a slightly darker smudge against the monsoon sky.

Arunachala is 2,682 feet high. It's called a hill and it's called a mountain. I slipped from one to the other, for neither term seems to contain it.

They say there's no need actually to set eyes on Arunachala. Simply thinking of it can bring liberation from the cycle of life and death. Here it was, after all my travels. Arunachala appearing as a thought form.

I stepped from my hotel for the first time, crossed between the rickshaws, bikes and people of the main street, and walked down the colonnade of shops that leads toward the main gateway of the temple. Every walk out into these streets of Tiruvannamalai would be a mission out of the confines of myself.

"Hello. You are going to visit.....?"

I didn't catch the name of where I was supposed to go, but looked at my guide instead. His robe was fulsome, a wrapping of bright orange cloth tight around his lean frame. More bright orange wrapped a thin turban round his head. His beard was long and black and full, though he was young.

He spoke again of who he thought I should see. It was a man and not a place. A small laminated photo of him was on sale in a store at the temple gates. He looked robust and elderly, a green turban and grey beard framing his head.

I let myself be led away a short distance. Stone steps led up to an iron grille that formed a front door. Beneath the steps ran the channel of an open sewer. It was hard to see past the attendant and inside the house, for the windows were not glazed and garlands were stuffed between their iron bars. Their leaves now brown, they choked the windows of light.

People were let in one by one. My turn came.

Women in gold-trimmed sarees lined a wall inside, cross-legged on the floor and singing hymns to the saint composed of his name. It was a long name, so it was good to have it repeated again and again. I began to try and learn it.

"Yogi Ramsuratkumar. Yogi Ramsuratkumar. Yogi Ramsuratkumar."

The saint was elderly and seated on rush matting in the dark beyond of the room. His home was a hovel transformed into a cave. I saw the green turban, the grey beard, and sensed his head turn toward me as I sped past.

I nodded my head, a version of the embarrassed bob I manage in the aisle of Catholic churches, and followed the direction of a lady in ochre robes who sat opposite the saint. She leaned from the wall to flag me forward, and patted the patch of floor where offerings were placed.

I lowered a bunch of bananas to the ground and pulled apart the cradle of my hands to leave them there. My rite had played itself out. As I stood I had nowhere to go but outside. I backed away, nodding my head and holding my hands as though in prayer, then turned past the ladies in the doorway.

They waved their hands to stop me. There had been a call. The saint was asking for my return. He had two gifts for me.

One was the look from his eyes. They were an expression of light in darkness. I was happy to feel his compassion.

The second gift was a lump of crystallized sugar.

I carried it away, set it on my tongue in my room that evening and sucked till it melted and ran down my throat. I was happy for the juice to be a potion, and for it to do me good.

On rare occasions back home in Glasgow the sun had shone for several days at a time. Folk came out to street corners and stood blinking in the warmth. As the fine spell of weather persisted, characters changed. Bodies held in tight against the cold became expansive. Hands curved expressively through the air to conduct conversations. Voices swelled to call good humour to others across the street. The skies above Scotland became blue like heaven and Glaswegians laughed in the Mediterranean air.

The curtains of rain then blew back in to make mirrors of the pavements, which reflected a dark sky. It was a dream, this time of being opened by the sun. Doors of tenement apartments slammed shut to close people inside, and they took shots of whisky to remember the time of warmth.

Inhabitants of colder countries grow into solitude. It's the way we've learned to live, so we're sure it's morally superior. Western progress stems from such solitude, such independence.

There's proof for this view in the natural world, for those who need it. Keep a seedling away from sunlight by sealing it in a closet, and it sprouts high. The plant is very pale, of course. And though its height is magnificent, it lacks the strength to keep itself alive.

It's fine to grow indoors for our early years. Then we have to open our doors and learn to step out with the world.

My first steps to saints and sacred mountains were awkward, as first steps always are.

Stepping out on the road that hugs the base of Arunachala, travelling westwards, I soon left the press of the town's low white buildings behind. In town I was the only obvious foreigner, but out here was where westerners roamed. Through intense spiritual practice sets of blinkers had been trained to grow out of the ether and shield their eyes. Ghostly white, often lean and tall, these spiritual aspirants ignored the life to the sides of them and stared straight ahead. A refusal to look at India allowed them to walk in an invisible world.

Much of this area houses the ashram built around the final home of Ramana Maharshi. Scores of beggars were waiting on the road outside; they were the limbless, the albino lady with mottled skin, abject people in their ochre robes. Hands were held out, bowls rattled, imprecations whined. Their role at this spiritual centre was to accept charity as a service to others.

I left my shoes at the ashram entrance and walked barefoot through the gate.

By the wall of the ashram's original assembly hall I looked through its iron bars. A life-size statue of Ramana has been placed before the couch where he habitually sat. Made of dark metal, naked but for a cloth tied by a string around its waist, the statue sits cross-legged on a pedestal.

The grounds of the ashram are studded with tombs of early devotees. I passed a final four, dedicated to Lakshmi the cow, Jacky the dog, a crow and a deer. Beyond the tombs a small signpost pointed an arrow up a slope toward a gate, and so on to the mountain's slopes. "Skandashram 1.4km ". A path led up to Ramana's original ashram on the mountainside.

Arunachala was warm to the touch. The path of golden rocks was laid by devotees of Ramana for his daily walk on the hillside. I trod in his footsteps. The rocks were as rounded as tortoise shells with a warmth as of life inside them.

My visit had come at the tail end of a healthy monsoon. Rains had soaked into the mountain that was formerly red, bathing it after five years of drought. Green shoots sprouted through the ground.

A game was played around my feet. Miniature butterflies danced there for a while, and I noted their patterns and colours before they flitted away. These were the rules: a point was mine if I managed to match butterflies into a pair, and a point went to the butterflies for every specimen they flew in that stayed an individual of its species. It was a delightful game to lose. I loved to draw butterflies as a child, colouring pages with the symmetry of their wings, but the inventiveness of this hillside has only ever been matched in the freedom of dreams.

When I had no crayons I used to make do with a pencil, and here she came too, the butterfly of those sketches, her black wings patterned with broad white spots.

Tiny lizards played a trick. A stripe down their sides narrowed and took on colour to form a bright red tail. This tail pointed one way, while they darted off in another. A cricket was striped in yellow and blue, large and still in the way the butterflies are small and fleeting, the wings of its back running green and mottled toward a burnished tip.

Perhaps all ground has pleasures like these if I learn to watch my feet more carefully.

The Skandashram was Ramana Maharshi's home for many years, before his mother's old age and infirm legs brought them all down to the base of the hill. The ashram building is low, built in trim blocks of white stone raised on steps above the ground, with a red tin roof and a run of green shutters and doors. An attendant beckoned me inside. At the back of the building, through two rooms, a small chamber had been turned into a shrine to Ramana. A rush mat was laid down in front of his photograph, a fragment of firelighter puffed into flame on a salver, and ash was smeared on my head before I was left to meditate.

There is a courtyard outside, paved and surrounded by a low wall. The site is an oasis of trees that drop down mottled shade. Their leaves discovered a breeze and rustled. I sat down, crossed my legs, and breathed in the stillness of the place.

There is another, still earlier retreat of Ramana's to visit on an alternative way down the mountain; the Virupaksha Cave. This is named after a saint of around four hundred years ago, drawn to the hill from the neighbouring state of Kerala. When he was old and about to leave the body he asked his devotees to leave him alone for the night. They returned the next morning to find just a small pile of ash. The saint had died and made a tidy cremation of himself. Because of the sacredness of Arunachala it is not possible for anyone to be buried on the hill, so he had taken the only way of ensuring he could remain there forever.

It is a pleasant place, fronted by a green entrance gate and a whitewashed patio. A small stone lingam (the phallus-shaped stone sacred to Hindus) was honoured with rose petals, a tree dropped pools of shade, and a low white building had been built across the front of the cave. It was tended by a middle-aged Mexican sannyasin in white robes, his head balding but with a fine bush of grey beard. The outer room was bare of possessions but for photos of Ramana around its walls, and books to be borrowed by devotees which rested on a stone couch that Ramana built.

The inner cave is said to be the shape of Om, the root sound of all creation. Unlike most shrines it had not been blackened by smoke and ghee, and the contours gave me a sense of sitting in a large, pale eardrum. Red roses were piled in a mound on an altar of black bricks, before a picture of Ramana. Ramana himself had fashioned the pile of Virupaksha's ashes into a lingam.

A western devotee was already installed on cushions. There was a lustre to his pale skin, and a stateliness to his pose. He out-sat me, but I was intrigued enough to sit outside till he emerged. He slipped into blue rubber sandals, slotted black spectacles onto his nose, and hooked a black brolly over his arm. The body that was erect in sitting was paunched now he was standing. He looked like a junior in a minor London bank on an outing to an office toga party. The spots on his young face screamed red at the sunlight as he padded off for his downhill walk.

I had a friend at university who went on to become a concert pianist. His body was angular and awkward, his skin a blotch of nerves, but the instant he arranged himself above a keyboard he was transformed. His manner and physique were electrified by genius. In the western devotee I had watched the process in reverse. His ordinariness was transformed by meditation.

His family in Europe probably grieved for his loss. In fact it is a miracle of the wide range of options the world has to offer, that he was able to find his vocation in a small Indian cave.

Arunachala can shimmer as a shadow. It can blaze red. It can dust itself green. It can vanish altogether, so that from the sun-baked town of Tiruvannamalai at its foot you cannot see it at all, only sense its presence.

Arunachala is a mountain that rises from the plain in this southern Indian state of Tamil Nadu, but it is clear that it is also something else. Here is what a sacred Hindu text, *The Skanda Purana*, has to say about it:

Two of the great trinity of Hindu gods, Brahma and Vishnu, were quarrelling about which was the greater. Shiva, the other member of the trinity, had supremacy as so much a part of his nature that he felt no need to compete. Instead he appeared before the two warring gods as a column of light and set them a challenge; whoever was able to reach the end of this column would be deemed supreme.

Brahma took the form of a swan to fly up to the top, while Vishnu became a boar to burrow his way down to the bottom. He thrust in his tusks and charged through layer after layer of the Earth but the column of light remained always as strong beside him. Spent with exhaustion, Vishnu surrendered and gave praise to the almighty power of Shiva.

Meanwhile Brahma's wings grew ragged as he spiralled up and up toward the top. His flight dwindled and he knew he could go little further when a leaf floated down toward him. He recognized it as a leaf from the tree that grew on the summit of the light, plucked it from the air with his beak, and flew with it back to Earth as proof that he had reached his goal.

Before the might of Shiva it was impossible for him to sustain the lie. Brahma confessed. Vishnu won some laurels for his greater humility, but the two gods' rivalry was drained of significance. They were both consumed with a longing to fall in adoration before Shiva. This was impossible however, for the column of light was too bright to behold. The gods begged Shiva to assume a kinder form. He consented, and became a mountain.

The mountain is Arunachala.

That no-one should forget the source of the mountain, Shiva vowed that he would reappear as this column of light on one day every year. This was to be on the full moon in the Tamil month of Karthigai, which bridges November and December. An annual festival heralds the appearance of this beacon, or *Deepam*, on the summit of the mountain.

This annual festival was in three weeks time. No longer shy of festival crowds after the wonders of Ireland, I was determined to stay and enjoy it.

The Skanda Purana gave me clear instructions on how to respect Arunachala whilst walking around it. I should walk clockwise, treading as carefully as a queen in her ninth month of pregnancy. I must not cover my head against the sun, nor protect my feet from the ground.

And so I started in the early morning, before the sun was high. And I bent down to take off my sandals and go barefoot.

As I stood up, an old man had appeared and stood in front of me. I intended to go up the trail that he had come down so I went to my right. He went to his left. I moved to my left, he to his right. He blocked my way and grinned.

He had a face to smile back at. Slightly smaller than me, he was higher up the path so our faces were at the same level. His stance was as serene as a fashion model's pose on a catwalk. Apricot cotton robes were wrapped tight about him like a winding sheet, a length of it drawn up as a cover for his head. His grey hair hung in waves. His beard curled from its thick moustache, the grey yellowed with nicotine, to drop down to a point far below his chin. His face was narrow with high cheekbones, little crow's feet of attention beside his eyes. The most curious aspect of him was his teeth. They were large and yellow, glued in at separate angles, the middle three missing from the top row. In almost any other face it would be difficult to see beyond such a display, but it was only later that I noticed them at all.

"Mountain?" he asked, bending slightly and arching his head to follow the course of his arm as he looked up toward Arunachala's summit.

I explained that I was walking around the mountain and not up it.... "No. Round," I said, as I held up my fist and walked a circuit through the air with the fingers of my other hand. Our conversation was to rest on the limits of his English and the non-existence of my Tamil, yet it served us well enough.

He held a hand in the air, thumb and fore-finger pressed together, pinching hold of the moment and so conjuring all of my attention. I watched the hand dip into his cotton bag and come out holding a lemon, perfect in form and brightness and only an inch high. This he placed on a rock beside the path. With fingers of both hands now, he walked around it.

The lemon was the mountain, one pair of fingers was himself, the other was me.

"You, me, round," he said. "Come!"

He stepped around me. I wanted to carry on up the mountain path, presuming to find a soft and dusty pilgrim trail shaded by trees.

"No, no. Come!"

And so I learned that no separate trail existed. Pilgrims shared the main road with traffic.

I trod along by his side. His name was Swami Annamalai. He lived on the mountain where he was the guardian of the Parvati temple, Parvati being a goddess and the consort of Shiva. He looked down at my bare feet and laughed, then padded on ahead in his blue rubber flip-flops.

Lorna, my erstwhile Scottish girlfriend, was big on footwear and survival gear. She would head out on even a modest hike as though scaling the Himalayas. It was her way of respecting the mountains, knowing that weather could always turn and safe ground become treacherous. Were she with me now I would have been kitted out. We would have sprinted to the top of Arunachala before breakfast and enjoyed the view.

Lorna, however, was striding through a different land and I was trying to live by a different set of rules. Arunachala was not there to be climbed, the *Skanda Purana* told me. Circumambulation was the proper way of showing respect. I looked down at my bare feet, which Lorna had once claimed to love, and felt a twinge of love for them myself. A bed of dust was gathered to either side of the road. The tensions in my body began to ease, the dust nursed my feet toward comfort, and the walk switched from penance to pleasure.

Land and fields separated us from the mountain's base. From town Arunachala has the shape of a pyramid, but like Croagh Patrick a run of lesser hills gathers like a spur to its side. This walk would be a long one. We had no time for detours.

A sandy lane cut to the right from the roadside and headed straight toward the hill. "Siddhasramam," Annamalai said, and nodded down the way. "Kattu Shivan. Very good ashram."

Did I want to go down there? I saw the stones that filled parts of the path, and checked that it wasn't on the actual route of the pilgrimage. It wasn't. It was a detour.

"Later," I declared. "Another day."

I walked on, at a pace dictated by a queen's pregnancy, but for each of my steps Annamalai took only half a step. He leaned his head forward to stare at my back, then swivelled it round to look toward Kattu Shivan.

"Do you want to go?" I asked.

His eyes stayed still, watching me, as his head nodded.

I turned and retraced my steps. He grinned.

The swami grew excited and gained speed.

"Refectory," he announced, breaking into a trot.

He was hurrying to a square of crumbled earthen walls.

"Tank," he said, and showed me the stone steps that led into a round pool filled with water. It used to be the peaceful heart of the ashram. To the right of the tank was a section of white wall.

"Temple," he said, and bowed down. His eyes moistened as he

led me on a track through woodland to the place where his parents once lived. Cattle were ripping grass from between the stones of its ruins.

Annamalai had brought me to his childhood home. He was born here. His parents worked the ground, tending the gardens and buildings. He was their son, and he could make the place grow again. With money he would rebuild the ashram and set his own name above it -- my name too if the money he received came from me. He stood in a grove, the sacred mountain behind him, and recited a litany of the countries from where the money might flow -- Italy, Japan, Germany, America, France.

Kattu Shivan means Shiva of the jungle. It is the name that was given to the holy man who formed this ashram around himself. He meditated in a cellar beneath the little house devotees built for him. On the first day of each Tamil month many devotees drove out of town on bullock carts to pay their respects. They passed a sign that read 'No Protestation here!' for Kattu Shivan led a stern life. He wore a basic loincloth, claiming the orange robes of sannyasins were mere self-advertisement, and refused ornamentation such as the grey lines of ash which worshippers of Shiva stripe across their foreheads.

I asked the Swami how many years the ashram had been abandoned and he reached down to write 30 in the sand. Later, when I asked him his age, he reached down and drew the figure 67.

We paused on the path on the way back to the road, beside a light brown stone somewhat shorter than a man that was hidden behind a thorn bush.

"Is this a good stone?" I asked, ready to believe it sacred.

"Good stone," Annamalai confirmed, and bowed his head.

(I came out this way on a later walk, along a tracery of tracks past cactus trees and over streams, and discovered the stone was in fact a termite hill, but didn't begrudge the swami his game. I was keen to be pulled into the drama of the moment, wherein everything was sacred.)

Annamalai faced me and started to sing. His voice was strong and pure, pitched high. I understood I was to sing with him, and was surprised how many notches my voice had to move up before I had a tone akin to his.

"Arunachala Shiva," he sang, then so did I. With the words secure I worked on the tune, the same line evenly pitched but ascending, then doing little swoops and glides for the fourth rendering. He gazed into my eyes all the time, his own a soft brown, for in teaching me the song he was giving me the twin names of his god.

I practiced, repeating his phrases, then we sang in unison before moving on to other verses with more complex lyrics. As I faltered or made a mistake he spoke the correction and on we went.

Suddenly he looked stern. I was puzzled, then saw that this was some pantomime he was playing to lead me to an understanding. Aspirants must come to Shiva in the right manner (and it was for this that he looked solemn, bowing down and padding a few steps on the spot), then Shiva (he stood erect to become the God, inflated his cheeks till their skin was taut, then sent the air rushing out through the trumpet of his lips), Shiva would blow the wind of his power into them.

He tilted his head to stare at the summit of Arunachala that rose behind my back.

"Come in, Shiva," he intoned, and we both stood with our hands clasped and eyes closed for a few moments.

"My boss, come in," Annamalai breathed.

We opened our eyes, smiled, and resumed the sacred way.

Two green parakeets sported themselves around the dark dome of a building on our left. This houses the Nirudhi *lingam* (a lingam being the phallus-shaped stone that is an image of God). This is the south-western of the eight lingams that mark compass points all around the hill. A statue of Nandi the bull is seated before the lingam in the dark interior, the bull signifying that the god Shiva is inside.

In the shade of the covered forecourt sat an old sadhu - "old man" his younger companion advised me, and I imagined he sat because his legs were too withered by age to support him any longer. Streaks of grey ash, the signs of a devotee of Shiva, marked the bald dome of his head, though his hair still grew as one long black tassel behind him. A large conch filled with ash sat by his side, and he bid me kneel down to have my forehead smeared with it.

He wished to adorn Annamalai too. The swami gave his excuses, and winked at me as we left.

Ancient stones were positioned along the way, supposedly at twenty minute intervals, but they were taking twice as long in coming round for us. I had reckoned on finishing the walk before darkness. If we kept a steady pace and avoided diversions, we could still do so.

The swami was in no such hurry. This next town contained a temple I must not miss. Its walls were the grey of an elephant's hide, its front gate somewhat larger than an elephant. He led me through it.

The temple's name was Adi Annamalai, in some ways the feminine counterpart of the vast temple in town. I was less able to see how it was unique than how it reflected all the temples of the region. We crossed the courtyard and entered the gloom of the main hall of worship. This was the home of various gods, housed in niches and either golden or blackened with the smoke of devotional flames.

The swami called to me. He looked most solemn. Ash was gathered in the creases of his palm. He brought pinches of it up to draw horizontal lines on my forehead, his lips fluttering in prayer.

Some creatures, swallows or bats, darted across the ceiling in the darkness behind the central shrine. I stood in some wonder, and tried to distinguish them by their shape in the swiftness of their movement. The swami tugged at my elbow. My wonder was misapplied. In the deeper darkness of a small shrine a statue of Shiva was standing hidden and required my full attention. I must clasp my hands in front of me like so, and intone after him.... "Shiva, Shiva."

Our chant inspired the swami. The next statue of the God we met showed Shiva as a dancer. Annamalai lifted his knee, splayed his fingers in the air, opened his eyes wide and froze his face in a smile, till the whole posture melted in his laughter.

"Dance," he said. "Shiva. Dance!"

A young sadhu passed us by, his bare chest ringed with beads, a greying cloth tucked around his waist. Ahead of us a narrow track cut off to the right, heading directly toward the mountain. The sadhu was thrilled. He tripped a dance on his heels and turned to face it, flinging his hands with their metal bowl high toward the heavens and stretching his body so that his skeleton pressed against his flesh.

A young boy carrying a bucket up the track shuddered to a halt and looked behind him, in fear of what might have caused such a gesture of surrender. He saw the mountain of Arunachala, knew such a gesture was appropriate, relaxed, and carried on.

The sadhu bowed low in a farewell prayer and turned back to the road. His slender fingers combed back the thick black tresses of his hair then splayed out at a level with his shoulder, held so that the nails shone in the sun. His hips swayed, he stepped high on his toes, and minced along the sacred way.

He was a model of ecstasy.

A lady sadhu passed us by, for we were still treading slowly. Her head was shorn down to a fuzz of black hair. She was clothed from neck to ankle in coarse brown cloth, a bag tucked under her arm, her face filled with a smile.

Two ladies in saris, taller than the lady sadhu as mothers are to a child, held up their arms to spread the material of their clothes like a barrier across the path. The sadhu, her face still eager with delight, looked up to where they pointed and listened to their tale. She clasped her hands and held them tight against her chest as she took in this new wonder of the mountain.

A symbol of Shiva is the crescent moon he wears above his brow. Some sunlight was still caught in the sky, but the blue was switching to grey. The ladies were pointing to the new moon that shone there as the thinnest sliver of itself. Its crescent, a pale gold, balanced above the summit of Arunachala till a wisp of cloud took it from sight.

That wisp was a herald of the evening. It brought in a mass of black cloud to obscure the hill before the rapid onset of night could seal it away in darkness.

We joined the press of the main road, the blaring of coaches pushing their way into the bus station, the lorries belching fumes, the auto rickshaws blurting daft noises from their bull horns, and pedestrians filling every space between. The temple of the goddess Durga, the primary Goddess of the town who once won a victory against fierce demons on the mountain, was lit with coloured lights. The temple's buildings are detached from the street by a flight of stone steps and the still space of its courtyard. Annamalai turned a tight circle on the roadway, chanting Durga's name, then led me on beyond the traffic of the town and down an alleyway toward the main gate of the great temple.

Our walk around Arunachala was almost complete. We stepped the final yards across the flagstones of the temple courtyard and down to the sacred tank. Its waters washed the dust from our feet. Fat carp streamed up to kiss our toes.

I agreed to visit the swami in his own small temple on the hill on the next day. He sat on the steps of a shrine and blinked with tiredness as I walked off to my bed.

Solitude is a great curiosity in India. Like the shell of a snail to a thrush Indians peck away at it, knowing there is something much juicier inside.

As indeed there is.

I smiled at the puzzled looks of small children, and was dazzled by their eyes as round and wonderful as planets and their teeth that smiled and shone with whiteness as they responded.

I let some people guide me to favourite places in town, and resisted others.

I put money into thrusting hands, but not into most. A youngster, with a shaven head as slender as a deer's and orange robes that stirred sounds with the wind of their movement, smiled and held out cupped hands. I shook my head, waiting to be asked once again. The youngster's head tilted to one side, the face flushed with a smile, and was gone. I ran to find him or her in the crowd, for I didn't know the sex of this human creature, but I found no trace. The sprite was gone.

The temple in town is vast. It might help to think of the Vatican rather than simply Saint Peter's for a comparison when assessing its scale. This is a walled and magnificent temple compound exclusive to gods. Different gods within the Hindu pantheon each have their separate temple home within the complex, while the acres of flagstones between them are polished to a shine by the barefoot feet of pilgrims. A sequence of gopurams, mighty towers dense with mythological sculpture, rear above each entrance way. Inside the high walls there are pools, there are gardens, and there are residential quarters for the servants.

And there is plenty of room for a temple elephant. She stood under a stone canopy, the bridge of her trunk like gold dust where grey skin had peeled away to reveal pinkness beneath. This very moist trunk reached out to siphon coins from pilgrims, then formed a graceful curve to slobber over their faces and tap them on the head.

It was an anointing. A blessing.

The temple has a series of gates that are familiar from fairy tales, each one the size of a giant's castle door. A final gateway gives admission to the heart of the complex. In the story of Arunachala, Brahma and Vishnu learned that even the great gods must know their rank. This heartland of the temple compound is where the principle deities are housed, central among them being the god Arunachaleswara. He is gracious enough to lend his name to the whole temple. A colonnaded walkway leads between the various gods' homes.

The slopes of Arunachala rise above the rear wall. The buildings are white, the mountain green, the sky blue, so that everything soothes and nothing startles the eye. Begging is forbidden within this inner courtyard. That is one reason this was a favourite place of mine. It was a relief to sit there and be free from demands for a while.

I sat and watch a young man. His dhoti was pulled up and tucked in around his waist so he could run. A vast salver covered with a silver dish was held above his shoulder, riding the stream of warm air on this flight from the temple kitchens and across the courtyard to the doors of the central shrine.

This was lunch time for the Gods. The meal was hot, and must not be late.

Shiva and Parvati are fully represented by their gold statues. They have a bedroom in their shrine, to which they are carried at night. The curtains are drawn back in the morning and the gods are brought out for their breakfast. Whenever I spent time in this great temple it was a regular shock to hear the hammering of drums, the blasts from long horns, and meet one of these golden statues, their throne resting on poles stretched across men's shoulders, racing about the precincts on their daily round of exercise.

It was a game, but one more vital than life. The Gods must tour their domain, must eat before their servants do.

I trod the path up the mountainside on my visit to my new friend the swami. The temple in town is measured in acres, while the one I was headed for could be measured in spans of a hand. To understand this new scale of things, please imagine this:

Mother has lived with you all of your life. Long as that is, it is nothing. She was here long before you were born. She's a big woman, as dark as you are pale, as heavy as you are light. Her body is cold and gives nothing to the touch when you come in to change her dress. Her clothes -- gold, yellow, blue, red, green -- hang on a line in the corner. You chose them for their brightness. They stretch across Mother like ribbons tied in a wind.

Visitors you have never met come to pay their respects. They stand in silence and look over your head. She stares back out of her gloom, and they go away.

The house has two rooms - hers at the back and yours at the front. Lie down and you span your room's length, lie the other way and you span its width. The walls are of bare cement but you have covered them with photographs of important people in your life, and of yourself. The ledge beside the floor where you sleep holds your six precious books. Your other belongings are on a shelf above the door. There's no internal door, so that Mother can look out on every aspect of your life.

This is the home of Swami Annamalai, only the Mother is a statue of the Goddess Parvati and this home is her temple on the hill. Its white flat roof is decorated with a sculpted lotus flower and two squatting, passive bulls.

The Swami laughed in welcome and sat me down in his front chamber. A few shouts brought tea in metal tumblers.

"Parvati," he said, and pointed a finger at the steaming, spiced liquid. The tea had no milk, and needed none. It was made from the water that runs in a stream, past the house to gather in the tank below. The water in this stream is white. It is viewed as milk which runs from the goddess Parvati's breasts.

I sipped this mother's milk. It passed through my body to pour out as sweat, for this chamber was hot. I peered through at the goddess in her back room, looked at the books, and admired the photos on the wall. One showed a young man, his hair and beard a wild black tangle, his feet crossed behind his head.

This was Narayana Guru Swami, taken in his saner days when he was resident in the temple. For more than four years already he had been sitting on the mountain top, and only sitting. Neither standing nor lying nor walking nor crawling. Just sitting, in the one spot, day after day, season after season.

The swami and I planned our visit to him. Narayana only accepted food from the first people of the day to climb up to him with their offering, and if nobody came, he ate and drank nothing. The swami knew what food was welcome. Narayana liked tea, and so we must take that along with the accompanying sugar and milk. Other than that he ate monkey nuts, bananas and popcorn. The sum needed from me to provision our trip would be....

The swami tallied the amount in chalk on the floor.

Fifty rupees!

I queried this. I had to gorge myself with luxuries in my hotel to eat through twenty rupees worth at one sitting. We settled on forty and I handed the money over. We should begin our climb from his temple at five o'clock the next morning.

I queried the need for so early a start. He was sure.

Individual studs of light shone from small fires or lanterns on the dark mountainside. I imagined hermits in small caves, and wondered at their impatience for the light of day.

The swami was to have risen at four, sat and chanted his *Om* till his body hummed to its tune, and be glowing with his own light long before the dawn. It was the pattern of his every day. He would float up the black hillside like a firefly for me to follow.

Such was the myth. I found him asleep on his mat in the front room of his temple home. I sat outside and waited.

The Parvati tank was just below, its milk-water seeming to give off some light for I could make out the young men who gathered at its rim. They had borrowed the temple's metal bucket to haul up water, soaped themselves white, then upturned the bucket over their heads to stream themselves clean.

A hint of daylight caught white flowers on a bush. I moved to a seat on a boulder and watched this drama of light unfold on a broader scale. The first broad rays of the sun splayed a red backdrop to the town, still slightly grey and softened in mist. Strings of lights outlined the main tower of the temple, like a spacecraft anchored to the temple walls.

The swami called out for me at six o'clock. His wife had climbed down to the town and returned with the provisions. The weight of everything - bottles of water, milk, and the swami's filled yellow cotton bag - was stuffed inside my small pack and lodged against my back, and we set off.

The path was narrow and rocky. It led from immediately behind the Parvati temple to run as a steep brown channel up the hillside. We kept a slow but steady pace, the swami leading the way. Whenever my feet scuffed the ground, sent small stones scudding backwards, or made any other sound of haste, the swami's voice came back to still me.

"Oh," he lamented. "Shanti, shanti." His call invoked me to peacefulness, to calm, to walking with more care along this sacred way.

We barely paused. However we had to stop by water that had gathered in a mud pool. The swami divined that Arunachala had sent us this gift. The mountain was God. The water lay on the path as though cupped in God's own hands.

Eighty per cent of diseases in India are carried by water. I drank it bottled or boiled, peeled my fruit, and refused washed salad and ice cubes. I knew better than to stoop and sip water from a puddle.

"Arunachala," Annamalai insisted, and frowned to look as stern as an angry god while he spread out his hands in the sign of a gift.

I knelt down, scooped my hands in the puddle, sipped, then lifted some more for the swami to taste. His beard dried my fingers as he slurped my hands empty.

It tasted good. He wanted more. I bent to lift it and my hands stirred the mud. We watched the earth and water mix themselves in a swift whirling dance. The mountain was giving more of itself into the drink, but we accepted the limits of our digestive systems and climbed on.

The town below was awake now with the blare of horns from the bus station and the amplified music from its rooftops, but we had climbed beyond its noise into our own silence. There was just the scuffing of my sandals, the "Shanti, shanti" of Annamalai calling me to peace, and then the crashing of some creature hurling itself through branches.

It was a rhesus monkey. It hung single-handed from the branch of a lone tree across to our right, and surveyed us. It stayed silent as it watched, but more grunts and squeaks, a whole cavalry of fresh noises, chased themselves toward us from our left.

We were nearing the summit. An early rock of these final heights rose like a cliff to its smooth and rounded edge. First one face appeared, then another, and a whole stream of monkeys ran in to range themselves along the rock's rim and look down.

I had never felt so outnumbered. The swami walked on so I had to stay with him as the monkeys grunted their comments and squeaked their plans. They were too busy talking to follow us for now. We left the last of the vegetation behind and stepped on to the shoulder of bare golden rock.

The swami reckoned that Arunachala would not mind us stepping this far up its sides in our sandals, but this was the place to leave them behind. We buried them from the monkeys' sight beneath a thorn bush. I turned right to head for the summit. That is where my imagination had placed Narayana, sublime and exposed, bare skin on bare rock, eyelids closed as he spanned the Earth with each of the elements.

Instead the swami led the barefoot way back down the path, turning onto a track that disappeared between the greenery of bushes. He signalled that I should keep quiet. I followed him around a corner and into a clearing, where the monkeys had gathered in some form of parliament. They squatted on the boughs of a tree in the centre, on bushes, on surrounding rocks, on the earth, each turned to see what we had brought to their assembly.

To the left of the sloping path was a small hut, made of sticks, leaves, scraps of paper and plastic, just a few feet high and about five feet deep, one end open toward the town but with no real view other than the greenery that edged the clearing.

It took me a moment before I realized our man was inside.

We had to bow in order to see into his hut. Swami Annamalai took his rightful place in front of me.

The holy man's beautiful hands, with tapering fingers and traced with clear veins, reached forward to grab hold of the swami's right hand, tugging hard at the fingers, battling to daub them with ash as the swami tried to pull himself free, fingering ashy marks up the arms as well, the movements jerky, the swami shouting "Amma Amma" for the protection of his Goddess Mother and looking into the other's eyes in panic as he was pulled into the passion of the whole thing, the holy man talking back urgently, his voice the single note you make with your tongue pressed hard to the roof of your mouth, an urgent tone, like the desperate conversation of a mute. Ash streamed from his fingers as he reached up to daub more of it on the swami's head, then with a few strokes this decoration was complete.

It was my turn.

I knelt down and shuffled forward so as to be within reach.

I could see more than his hands now. I saw his face. It was young, surrounded by thick waves of black hair, a moustache curling upwards above the black shock of his beard, and his eyes black too, concentrating as he drew with ash upon my forehead, then reaching back for a thin garland of jasmine which he draped around my neck.

With this gift of a string of flowers the mood switched. He punched out his sounds, and flapped his right hand to shoo me out of sight.

I moved round to the path at the side of the hut, content to sit still while the swami undertook the business of offering our food. The monkeys tensed themselves. This was the ceremony that interested them most.

The milk came out first, poured from our bottle into coconut shells to be poured yet again onto roots at the base of the tree and over a couple of rocks, then more of it into a broken gourd set in the ground in the middle of the clearing.

This milk was worth a few sips to the monkeys, but no clamour. They were more into hors d'oeuvres than aperitifs. Swami returned the coconut shells to the wild man's hut and brought them back filled with a mixture of corn and nuts. Young monkeys flew like molecules as the food was scattered, their tiny hands flashing out for the pieces as they darted across the earth. The older and larger ones dominated a patch of ground to pick the food more slowly into their mouths, burned off some energy in chasing the smaller ones away, then ate again.

There were about forty of the creatures, individual characters with inquisitive expressions - young and old, large ones with red faces, an old lady with withered teats and one eye, two young males on top of a rock who shared a short high-pitched shout at the climax of a brief spot of anal sex. When the space grew quieter, when the food of our arrival had been cooked and passed around and swallowed, the monkeys grew still too. They sat picking each other for nits with their delicate fingers.

The mountain man had bound several sticks together with twine, so he could reach far out of his hut to swish at the monkeys or point out directions for the swami to run in. He now pointed the swami toward small stones. They were added to a pile kept at the front of his hut, ammunition to throw at monkeys and curious children.

Whatever else, it takes an immense discipline to sit without moving for year after year. I pitied this man, but that was stupid. You don't feel pity for an eagle in flight through a snowstorm. You marvel at its strength. Narayana sat in his mountain eyrie of tangled twigs, looked out with compassion then flicked moods to stab at us with his voice and hands, more obviously a man than an eagle but possibly more eagle than man.

He was certainly more at home on this mountaintop than I was. It was time to leave.

He piled more corn into each of our hands, and the rest was strewn in front of the hut. Nothing was stored. Unless secret treasures were woven into the fabric of his hut, Narayana's possessions seemed to be just a few pots and the clothes he was wearing. A knitted woolen scarf, fox brown, was wound about the top half of his body and the bottom half was covered in an old grey dhoti.

He broke the final banana into three for us to share, then beckoned me forward. I knelt for the final benediction, a fresh pattern of ash to be fingered on my brow, then I was urged back out of his sight. The swami knelt for his own farewell, and we left.

We paused on our descent for shelter inside a small cave - Ramana's Cave, the swami called it, with a low entrance but nicely rounded inside so that it was almost possible to stand straight. Apparently Ramana Maharshi used to sit on the rocks above and then come inside when the heat became too great.

The swami spoke of yoga, and was amazed that I had had a college education yet not studied this vital aspect. Now was a good time to learn. He showed with his hand the force rising from his groin to his head and went into a trance. When he came out of it, it was to tell me off - I was staring out through the cave's entrance.

"I give this to you!" he said, and demanded my concentration. I watched as he stared without blinking and stilled his mind. It was a very fine show of composure, followed by a mime of a typical westerner, eyes blinking like an owl's and head darting like a pigeon's.

We stepped from the cave and back into the glare of sunlight. The Swami took off the cloth protecting his head and wrapped it around mine, laughing at how good it looked and the fact that I needed it far more than he, an old man. The energy had been sucked from me by the sun, as though it didn't have enough of its own. I stumbled on

"Shanti, shanti," the swami said.

Back down at his temple he sat me in a large rattan hut as his wife brought in vessels of water from the Parvati tank below, then had me strip off down to my underpants and ladled water all over me. It was an honour, surprising and most refreshing. I was given an apricot-coloured dhoti to dry myself with, and another to wear. His wife then poured water all over the swami, and later I continued the work, the water coursing down the firm body of the old man so that it glistened.

A mat was laid out on the floor for me to lie on till food was brought, a large plate of rice and spiced green leaves. I picked at the grains, picked at the leaves, and nibbled away. I didn't know how to eat properly in this Indian mountainside fashion. The wife became a mother and I a child. She took away my plate and mixed it with her fingers. I ate well, with my knees crossed and the bowl on my lap. The wife, known as *Amma* or Mother by the swami, then washed my hand in a bowl, her fingers easing the dirt from my own. It was a joy to be so tended. She was a lovely woman, small, round-faced, quite old, her grey hair held back behind her head, elegant in a green sari that was a present from a Frenchman who visited every January.

The swami did not need to rest, but chatted at some distance to everyone outside. His voice broke through my doze. I lifted my head from the cushion which was set as a pillow beneath my mat, and drank a tumbler of tea. It was all very gracious and caring.

For a while, for as long as I chose, I had my home on the mountain.

For another aspect of life on the mountainside, beside Parvati's pool, I later sat on a low wall of the Ramana ashram to talk with another of the town's holy men. Westerners strode the street in front of us, like walking dead among lively Indians. Tall and white, their sights were trained on the ether. They say that any walk around Arunachala is made in the company of a host of holy spirits, souls who can think of no finer way to spend eternity than to walk round and round, round and round.

It is this same aura of divine greatness that brings many acknowledged holy people to this mountain. Mount Kailas, which many believe to be the world's holiest mountain, is simply the home of Shiva. Arunachala however is Shiva himself, his very embodiment, merged with the divine feminine in the form of Parvati. It is the pinnacle of the axis around which the world spins. Immersion in the River Ganges can break a believer from the cycle of birth and death. Such is the power of this mountain that simply to think of Arunachala confers the same benefit.

My new holy friend was Swami Narikutti. The world he left behind was an Australian one. He termed himself a Hindu monk and had been out this way for thirty five years, first working with his guru in Sri Lanka then coming to live in Tiruvannamalai. He was that curious white of a westerner, for which Orientals see us as ghosts, his bald head large and round and marked with tiny brown blemishes on the skin. He seemed truly poor. More money than he had saved had just been spent on a hip replacement in Madras, yet when a local sadhu creaked his body off the road to stand and deliver a life story he reached into the folds of his white robes and handed over some coins.

"He tells me he survived the wars," and Narikutti laughed. "The first and the second, and probably the Boer. But you see him. He is very old. Life here is tough for these people."

Swami Narikutti took his name from the jackal that kept him company during his many years in a hut on the hill. God had given him the mission to restore the Parvati pool, so for years he laboured to clear the silt and refresh the stone, living as a neighbour of Swami Annamalai. The care of his restoration work is still apparent.

The pain in his hip forced him down from the mountainside. His finances and ill health had sounded like a lament, so he smiled up at Arunachala and pledged his contentment. God and the hill were one and he was resigned into their care.

He spoke of the mountain.

"Yes, Arunachala is a lingam," he told me. "But take my advice. Do not take on the foolery of the world and think of it as a phallus. Of course it is that too, the lingam is a phallus, that's very clear. But it is also so much else."

He told a couple of penis jokes, but their humour turned on the subtleties of a Tamil pun so there was just his smirk and giggles for me to enjoy.

"To suck the phallus of the Shiva lingam," he carried on to inform me, with a lick of his lips, "you have to be very spiritually advanced. If you can understand the true nature of the lingam then you will have your understanding of sacred mountains. What is this secret? Only part of the lingam is visible, and the rest is rooted in the earth. It is the yogi penetrating the yoni, all that is male in life penetrating all that is female."

I thanked him, and stood to leave as he was tired.

"Where are you going?" he asked me.

"To Yogi Ramsuratkumar's ashram."

"Yogi Ramsuratkumar," he mused. "Everybody is going to see him. When he was young, you were lucky to catch him. Very lucky. What a fine man, what a great talker. Now he is old. His legs are gone. His devotees have him. Anyone can find him now. He can't get away. Off you go then, off you go."

He flapped a hand, half a wave of dismissal and half of farewell, and gazed back up the flanks of the mountain.

The Yogi's new ashram was projecting itself as buildings across a run of fenced off fields to the west of town. Within a year it would grow to have a domed meditation centre for four thousand people. For now the Yogi held audience in a temporary hall of rattan walls, bamboo supports and a thatched roof. With the crowds gathering in town for the upcoming festival, this was where to find him. He sat on a cement dais, his back framed by a plain grey stone.

It was a treat to see the Yogi in such clear daylight. His beard was long and straggling, the lips muttering beneath the nicotine-stained moustache. His dhoti was very off-cream, though his clothes were much cleaner than they used to be when his sleeves shone with the polish of dirt. His aversion to washing was total. He quoted the example of a local saint who pleaded 'no water, no water,' was washed in any case, had a stroke and died two days later. Bathing the Yogi was the equivalent of towelling a fish dry.

He smoked in a curious manner. The cigarette stuck up at an angle from his fingers as he formed a chamber of his hands in front of his mouth, the cigarette tip glowing bright as he inhaled, the dangers of passive smoking banished, for as the smoke curled toward his lungs he tended to raise both hands in benediction.

The Yogi's spiritual discipline was simple. He simply maintained the constant invocation that his lips were seen to mutter - "Ram Ram Jai Jai Ram." He used to live through begging, and it was as a beggar that he wished to be known - or perhaps as 'King of the Beggars'. It was only when he became seriously ill that he allowed devotees to buy him the hovel in town and this ashram outside of it.

A group of three ladies claimed the Yogi's special grace and offered him their home whenever he consented to use it. Their leader, Sri Devaki, sat at the Yogi's right hand during his public audiences. This young lady's face, quite chinless, was drawn back from enormous, pleading eyes. She used the Yogi's fan to keep him cool, staring up at his eyes or occasionally across at the devotees who gathered below.

When the Yogi was close to dying a few years back these ladies kept him in their home. They refused admittance to Rossaura, a Spanish devotee in Hindu robes who devoted her life to being near the Yogi's side.

"We don't want a beggar in this house," they told the Yogi.

"This man is a beggar," the Yogi replied, and ran away in the middle of the night.

People begin to line up to make their offerings, mostly of fruit. I pulled a tangerine out of my bag and tagged along at the back. Most prostrated themselves fully before him, and he slapped his blessing on their shoulder or head. The man before me buried his head in the Yogi's lap, and it took many slaps before he got up again.

My turn. I set down my tangerine, bowed down, then sat back on my knees. The Yogi had turned away for a fresh cigarette, and seemed surprised to see me there when he turned back. I wondered if he would slap me too, but his gift was sweeter. He gave me a quiet, delightful smile, a great charge of light and play in his eyes.

I returned to my spot on the floor, as my body hummed with its blessing.

Back in the temple forecourt in town a man held a thin chain. It was attached to the collar of a tiny monkey that was dressed like a bellhop in a red embroidered suit. It faced each of the smaller temple buildings that housed statues of the gods, and bowed low. The trick was helped by the trainer's fingers, which pressed down on the monkey's head. A small crowd stood in a ring round the monkey and laughed at every bow.

I watched the monkey and its senseless bowing to gods that held no meaning for it. I watched this little figure of fun, and I saw myself.

I sat in my room and wrote in letters home of how I could bring myself to bow before no more idols. The ritual round of a Hindu temple was an area that was closed to me, like Masonic lodges and molecular structures and the sky at night and the stock exchange. I had tried, the temple servants had welcomed me, but I could find no emotional way in. I sealed my letters, went down for dinner, and was proved sublimely wrong.

A young man was sitting in the dining room. He was striking in his composure, in his costume, and in his beauty -- the red spot and grey stripes of Shiva marked his forehead, and round his bare chest were long strings of glass and wooden beads, the orange Brahmin thread, and a beige cloth patterned like a leopard skin.

His companion beckoned me over. This man's name was Kannan. We had met in the temple one evening, when I was introduced around a group of friends gathered in their regular forum. He was here with this cousin, a Brahmin priest.

Both men had soft beards of young black growth. Kannan was in training at the local college for a business career. His clothes were western. He practised command over the waiters and criticized the food, for he was a good man bred to be self-confident and he had to keep checking himself against his environment to see how well he was doing.

The young priest checked himself against nothing. He contained a great stillness to him, though an initial wariness sheltered his black eyes.

Then he spoke through his cousin. He reached out to take me by the hand. I was invited to go with him to the temple.

His name was Arunachala, the same as the mountain. Apparently it is a usual name to give boys in this Indian state of Tamil Nadu, but to me it was special.

You cannot choose to be a Brahmin priest. You are born into the role. Your authority is not gained in this single life, but in a span of generations. Like one bead on the Hindu rosary, a mala of 108 beads, your aim is not to stand out but to continue what has gone before and connect with what will come ahead, in a constant wheel of divine service.

This young priest called Arunachala did of course stand out. Few people emanate such stillness. They shiver with insecurities and needs. What I liked most was his combination of quiet authority and youth. And exceptional beauty. He led me round the temple because he wanted to share what was most exciting and tender in his life.

We bypassed lines of patient pilgrims to head straight for the presiding deity. He was housed within a small shrine at the centre of a vast hall that was stuffed with grey light. A flame had been burning in front of him for over a thousand years. This was the god Arunachaleswara. The supreme god Shiva compacted his majesty into the mountain of Arunachala. Here we find the power of the hill in a still more compacted form. The power of Shiva bears the name Arunachaleswara and appears as a black lingam, a cylinder of stone with a domed top that appears like a human head when garlanded and crowned in gold thread and precious cloth, guarded from behind by a five-headed cobra that rises out of the darkness.

This is the stone that Ramana Maharshi hugged to himself. Ramana was an example of how it is possible to compact the immensity of this lingam still further, to take it inside and realize it as the self.

The young priest named Arunachala brought me the plate of sacred ash from before this god and decorated my forehead, then led me off to a corner shrine where Shiva and Parvati stood in a golden, human form. The ritual here was more elaborate. Leaves were heaped onto a salver and long incantations made over it, to include my name and those of my family as I lay my fingers on the salver's edge. A flame was then lit before the gods and brought back for me to pass my hand above its heat. The lines on my forehead were marked with new ash, and I accepted them as a very true gift.

Outside again we crossed the rear courtyard, this most exclusive area of the Arunachaleswara temple complex, and entered a grand building that was the closest the temple reaches to the holy mountain's side. Rich decoration is painted across its wooden ceiling, and richest of all is a display of gods ranged on a stage at one end. Beautiful images in golden metal, this is a version of the holy family to be paraded through the temple and onto the streets beyond.

Shiva and Parvati take centre stage. To their sides are their sons Ganesh, the elephant god, and the second son known in Tamil Nadu as Murgan; and to their right is a very pleasing figure from the 16th century, about two feet high, right hand held with the palm to face us, golden lips relaxed within a round contented face. This is Chandikeshvara, the family's bodyguard. It was toward this god that in his role of priest Arunachala was to focus the devotion.

Crowds, from babies to the very old, filled the temple and pushed against the ropes that shielded the ceremonial space. The materials for the *puja*, the offerings to the gods, were arranged on five wooden tables. Arunachala stationed me beside the rope, and devotees pushed in front to force me backwards. He took my hand again, lifted the rope, and settled me on the floor of the ceremonial space beside his nephew. His mother and sister watched from steps at the side.

Arunachala's assistant was an older, stouter Brahmin, a white dhoti wrapped around his waist like a towel in a steam bath, the rest of him glowing with sweat. He lifted a salver toward the statue, tilted the cover of the metal dish so the god could peep at his dinner, then stationed himself beside the table.

A silver lamp was circled in layers with many wicks, each of which was set to flame, and the set of silver instruments was ready to hand to Arunachala at the appropriate moment. These instruments were small models, intricately wrought, of a parasol, mirror, fan, emblem, fly-whisk and flag. Each seemed designed to balance the finest of gestures. The congregation let out their cries and raised clasped hands into the air as trumpets blared, drums beat, bells rang, and fans waved to blow the smoke and scents from incense, lamps and camphor around the devotees and their gods. Arunachala looked to his left, keeping pace with the puja of the other priests, intoning his words with their words, bearing the instruments through their formation dance of silver.

The temple hall was vast, the beams of its ceiling rich with the deep colours of the illustrations of divine stories. The crowds and musicians roared their love and shook with excitement and the beautiful gods glowed inside their gold.

The roar was the strength of devotion. With a love as strong as this you must be vulnerable. This vulnerable, fragile side of love was set before the feet of the gods. I saw it in this young man Arunachala, then focused again to find it centred in the movements of his wrist and hand. The wrist moved each instrument through its spaces in the air and fingers swept patterns within the clouds of incense. The gestures had been learned and performed by many generations, but I could see how they need never be stale. These gestures found fresh life in the muscles of the young man's arm. It was great artistry, given to the divine. I watched that hand, and the veins that pulsed down the arm, and was brought as close as I could ever hope to the gods of India.

The puja ended. The instruments were passed out of the hall, the tables pushed aside, and the gods raised on their carrying poles to be bounced off on their jaunty parade through the town. Arunachala's mother and sisters smiled down at him from the steps behind the altar. Arunachala handed me a couple of small bananas, *prasad* from his god.

"Very beautiful puja," he said, and smiled.

"Very beautiful," I agreed, and knew that nothing more beautiful could ever be shared. Others from the crowd reached for my bananas as we were crushed through the main doors, old ladies and men stroking my fruit with long fingers from thin hands.

The monsoon was sweeping the temple acres with its latest torrent. I opened my umbrella and we splashed side by side across the flagstones.

The streets grew more full with each day of the festival. The driver of a bullock cart offered me a lift from my hotel to the edge of town. I sat cross-legged on the bare wooden platform and was paraded along the high street. People saw me and laughed. I was both incongruous and exotic.

I looked forward to the arrival of a traditional Indian freak show in town; naked fakirs with arms paralyzed in the air, or the bed of nails stuff of the fairground. It never arrived. A man with a dagger through his mouth walked around the streets, but he was lonely. The festive air brought stalls to the main streets, some with large balloons or balls on elastic, others stacked with cut flowers, plus the general stalls of a local market where families came to browse. This was not a forum for the weird and the wayward. It was a family occasion.

It was good to see large numbers of women on the streets, gloriously bright in their saris. I walked through the Arunachaleswara Temple and watched them wheel their colours round and round the small temples.

It cost money to get in to the central shrines now, but the temple stayed open throughout the night and all of its buildings were full, pilgrims carpeting the floor with their bodies to sleep out of the monsoon rains.

People gathered on a building's steps to stare through the wooden slats of the gate at the elephant locked inside. The crowds and noise proved too much for her. As Shiva hurtled past on one of his processions she lifted her chained leg and trampled an old lady to death. The keeper and a guard were badly injured. It was thought best to remove her to a nearby jungle and find a baby elephant to replace her.

A big wheel span on an electric fairground near the temple walls, its lights flashing to amplified music. The shouts of children motored the version on a waste ground near my hotel. The families who usually slept there, bedding down at 6pm as night fell, had been moved to allow this fairground to come in. Children sat in wooden boxes and a man cranked them round in their wheel till they were hoisted to twice the height of their parents and squealed in delight.

You could hire a rifle to shoot at a board of deflated balloons, or visit the travelling zoo. An eagle was tethered next to the ticket seller. Animals were stacked behind a tarpaulin wall, geese and a fox with only bars in between them, two lions in separate cages with just room enough to turn their bodies around, a keeper rattling a stick between the cages of a mountain lion's cage to try and rouse it from apathy, a leopard pacing its cage, slinking its body first one way then the other to hold it back from the pressure of gaping people.

The most spectacular of the festival ceremonies saw what are known as temple cars pulled on a circuit around the outer walls. Chariots is a better name than cars, the wheels of the largest much larger than a man and with the power to turn and crush him, a broad base of intricately carved dark wood forming the tower of its base, and way up high a large pagoda of brightly painted columns in which one of the deities presides. Deep crowds lined the route as others filled the rooftops along the way, while a score of boys climbed up to keep the deity company and shrieked with laughter at the thrill of the ride. A man beside them raised his flag for the chariot to proceed and the men, in two lines packed tight in their hundreds, lifted links in chains that spanned their elbow to their hands, then the lines stretched and the chariot rolled, grinding the stones on the path to dust.

A bullock cart trundled behind, with a load of large wooden wedges to be thrust beneath the wheels as brakes till they splintered. And amongst the crowd walked young families, their new babies and infants swinging in slings strung from the leafy staves of sugar cane, travelling on the their first ritual circuit of the temple.

The chief priest of the temple, named Ganesh, selected me for another tour of the shrines. I had seen him earlier climb to reach up above the trunk of his namesake, a large silver image, and decorate this elephant god's forehead with a fine red spot before it was carried off on its tour of the town. Now my forehead too was spotted, after a fresh ceremony of flames before the shrine of Arunachaleswara.

I was presented before Parvati in the same way, in her shrine in the neighbouring *mantapam*, my heart beating fast as I was garlanded with a string of ballan leaves as thick as the circle of both of my hands.

I stepped out beneath the ghost tower (the gopuram nearest the hill) to the street behind the temple, and walked with the throng that was following the mountainous car of Shiva on its procession. Barefoot, my forehead decorated with a seascape of grey ash and the rising sun of my red spot, a forest of leaves around my neck, a jasmine flower in my hand, I was as ostentatious and as happy as a pantomime dame.

The walking route around the mountain was filled on the day of *Deepam*, the lighting of the beacon on the summit. Some walked in silence, others went high-stepping and singing songs in carnival groups.

More pilgrims traced a ribbon of white up the path to the summit of Arunachala. I had read that the object was to carry up ghee as fuel for the flames, and white linen to be used as its wick. The management of my hotel gave me a bottle filled with warm ghee, some linen wrapped in a brown paper bag, and the honour of carrying up this contribution from them.

"Is it OK to go in shoes?" I checked with the manager as I headed out of the lobby.

He wagged his head from side to side and forced a thin smile.

"It is not auspicious," he said.

I went back to my bedroom and left my sandals on the floor, along with my common sense.

I cannot write of how it feels to climb barefoot for others, only for myself. The walk around the mountain was level, with nothing more painful to tread on than grit. The ascent was composed of many sharp rocks. For me it was excruciatingly painful, every step a torture.

The hill's regular pilgrims, mostly men but a few women padding up the way in their saris, were surprised to see me and found me comical.

"Go, white man, go!"

"Hey, English *sami*!" sami meaning friend

"Foreign" was another label,

"Welcome" and spells of handshaking.

"What's your name?"

"How are you?"

"Happy Birthday to you!"

Plus whatever comments were passed in Tamil.

I had never felt old before, but did so there. One old lady, her back bent in a permanent stoop, tapped her way at speed down the hill, her stick giving rhythm to her chanting. Another was ascending, graceful in a dark blue sari, her silver hair in a bun, gazing up at the peak. Both were pointed out to me. "Great will," they had, they were an example. Hands pushed and pulled me up, sometimes grabbing both my arms to propel me so that I was both fast and powerless. It was horrible.

When I am truly old, let me go slowly or not at all. I shall have tired of speed by then.

Many noticed the blood that now coated my big toe. I smiled and looked rueful. I would be whizzing along were it not for my injury, I wished to imply, though the toe was merely stubbed and perhaps the least painful part of me.

The crowd was sharing the same joy in the day as the pilgrims on Croagh Patrick. For some reason I was apart from the mood this time, and could not share their joy. I was almost alone in my extreme discomfort, my distress.

One other man felt uncomfortable on the mountain. I heard later of Narayana Guru Swami, the holy man of the summit. He kept to the dark at the back of his hut and lowered his head, so that his hair fell forward to shield his face from the folk who peered inside.

I made it to the top, a summit now strewn with the litter of coconut hair and banana skins, and pressed myself into the tight file of men that lined up to drop a coin or simply stare into the base of the beacon to be lit that night - an empty copper drum that wobbled when touched. It was a crude object but holy. As with such objects on Croagh Patrick, the ritual thing to do was walk around it.

My vision of pilgrims bearing tubs of ghee and folds of white cloth was romantic and unfounded. They climbed empty-handed. The fuelling of the flame was a task allotted to a special caste of men, in their uniform of checkered dhotis and grey muscle shirts, towels wound round their heads in protection against the sun. The ghee was gathered in a circle of metal canisters and earthenware pots. I handed across the hotel's contribution.

"Five rupees," the attendant snapped. It was hot work on the mountain top. I handed over the fee.

Then it was off downhill again, for there was nowhere on top to rest. A man presented himself as my guide for the way down, a rare case of a man not barefoot but in sneakers.

"Slow, slow," he kept saying. "Follow me," and he grabbed for my hand. It was most irritating.

And the walk was so painful. Vaulting on rocks, sitting and dropping as carefully as I could, treading on the edge of balance, I knew I would make it in the end, for this was a lesson in disassociation from the body, in the knowledge that all things pass both good and bad, that everything in this life is fleeting....

It became so that I could not even stand still, my head spinning, urging me to fall.

At six o'clock I sat on the mountainside in the freshly gathered darkness. It was time for the lighting of the mountain. A shout went up from all those around as the town cracked fire, rockets shot high and fireworks burst white across the rooftops as strings of coloured bulbs lit the outlines of the temple. Power had flowed down from the mountain to crackle and spark as electricity across the plain. It was the whole Earth catching Arunachala's divine light.

I didn't see the deepam, the hilltop beacon, until I was down on level ground. It was good to see it from there, small and orange, a point of stillness against the sky.

The deepam was doused at nine o'clock the next morning, the flame disappearing beneath a spume of black smoke, then relit for a few hours at six. The crowds had gone from the temple. The elephant, made mad as elephants are by clamour and noise, returned. I climbed Coral Hill, in shoes.

The hill is within the eastern part of the town. It is dominated by a disused temple to the god known here as Murgan, the second son of Shiva. Its boulders and empty spaces are used for lovers' trysts after dark. I was looking for space to be alone and gather a final view of my stay.

I wondered how deeply the mountain had affected my life. A young man had sat opposite me in a restaurant one night and asked for spiritual guidance. He had started Transcendental Meditation, he told me. It had disturbed his balance of mind and was ruining his studies. Did I know of a spiritual practice that could blend with his way of life?

I recommended japa, the constant repetition of a holy name. It was as innocent and powerful a way as I knew at the time. I asked him if one holy name meant more to him than any other. He smiled and blushed, and said "Arunachala".

As I passed into sleep that night Arunachala repeated itself as a mantra inside my head.

It is believed that Arunachala is a wish-fulfilling mountain, that any wish you make here will be granted. True wisdom is to make no wish at all, for a wish amounts to karma and you are threatened with rebirth until it is played out. For all that, as I stood on Coral Hill and looked out at the mountain I found I was coming close to a wish for myself.

I looked at the form of Arunachala and wished to be like that, like a rock. I wished to be firm in my spiritual resolve and not be prey to desires, both my own and other people's.

I heard shouts. A group of schoolboys had spotted me and was running down the hill. I sat still and was surrounded. Their English was hesitant, and I had had so much strange company of late that I was shy of communicating at all. We were shy of each other. Then the more I spoke, the more they responded.

They were studying English poets in school; Wordsworth, Milton and Shakespeare. I could see their school if I climbed with them to the top of the hill, and they could point me round their whole town.

I joined them. We jumped over walls and climbed onto a rooftop to see what they had to show. I grew innocent again in their company. They charmed me out of my solitude.

"Happy Christmas," they said as they waved me back down the hill, though it was still a month away.

"Happy Deepam," I replied.

"Deepam's over," they said, for time moves on.

"Well just be happy then," I tried. "Happy for its own sake."

~~~~~~~~~~

"Ahh," Rossaura sighed, when she heard I was on a quest for sacred mountains. "Then you will be going to Tirupati next?"

Rossaura, the Spanish devotee of Yogi Ramsuratkumar, had pledged herself to Arunachala. Once she had found her way to this mountain she saw no sense in ever going anywhere else. In her memories though she often returned to the hills of Tirupati.

I had never heard of them.

"You have now!" she admonished me. "I have just told you about them. They are very near. Now you know about them, you must visit. Vishnu is waiting for you there!"
~~~~~~~~~~

4
The Hills of Tirupati
Tamil Nadu, India

Every good journey ends in friendship.

For the fifty thousand people a day who come to the sacred hills of Tirupati in southern India a good journey ends in a direct meeting with God, but that wasn't good enough for me. God is almighty. Almighty is not a quality of friendship.

I am picky about friends. I was travelling up the mountainside on the back of a doctor's scooter. We rode bareheaded in the sun, the scooter whined beneath our combined weight, and the doctor had given up his working day out of kindness. He was doing his best by a visitor to his town, yet I did not want him as my friend. I sensed no excitement in him.

Old red buses bulging with pilgrims squeezed past us on the narrow road. Their god took the form of a statue made in heaven, and had dropped himself into position on this sacred mountaintop. His name is Lord Venkateswara. When alive he was the tenth and last incarnation of the great god Vishnu, and might have made a good friend. Now people found comfort in his tall black stone image, and took spiritual renewal from his eyes.

I was yet to understand the Indian devotional absorption in objects of stone. That would come, as my journey took me closer to the essence of mountains. For the moment I was more intrigued by the man who appeared in posters on either side of the road. He looked alive. Wrapped in the orange robes of a Hindu monk he sat cross-legged at the heart of a giant lotus flower, a quiet smile on his face as he stared out. He looked young. He looked friendly.

I asked about him. It took several attempts to clear the barriers of language and scooter noise before I understood. His name was Sree Sree Tridhandi Srimannarayana Chinna Jeeyar Swami. As with all potential friends his name was ripe for shortening. Chinna Jeeyar Swami would do, but he was more popularly known as Swamiji. The previous October he had established his fame by hosting a spiritual festival on the mountain in honour of Lord Venkateswara. The mountaintop had blazed with candles and hummed with the chants of celebrating priests, while food was given to one hundred thousand pilgrims each day.

That was in October, but these posters looked fresher than that. A new festival, a Yaga, was being held on the plain to honour the female deity of the region, Ammavaru who was the consort of Venkateswara. A triumphal arch scripted the Yaga announcement in fairylights on the approach to the city of Tirupati below. The festival's host was Swamiji.

That was for later. The scooter continued to wheeze us up to pilgrim heaven.

The air at this altitude was cooler and so easier to bear, but otherwise the sense of a sacred hilltop was lost. It had been levelled and cemented into a town called Tirumula. Buildings were vast civic blocks. Some were hostels, some swallowed pilgrims by the thousands and gave them free meals, and the most imposing of all was a barber shop. Families trod down its flight of stone steps and had the sun reflect off their heads for the first time, parents and children shaved to a shine and their hair offered to their lord.

The main square was fringed with souvenir stores, peddlers selling coconuts, incense and flowers for offering, and families carrying baskets of provisions to wait in the perpetual line of devotees that rings the outside of the temple. They had come prepared for the slow shuffle through a maze of barriers that was expected to last for hours.

An alternative route took those with money around the wide and empty pool of the bathing ghat, through a maze of their own, and to a booth where tickets costing thirty rupees propelled them toward the beginning of the line. As an obvious foreigner the temple authorities asked me to sign a form assuring them of my respect for the majesty of their resident Lord. I did so truthfully. I respected him for prompting such a constant stream of devotion.

The temple exterior is grey, plain and low, surrounded by the caged walkway that contains its visitors. These Indian temples grow like a ripple from the central stone, the idol which has its home at the centre. Dark in the outer chambers, this temple grows brighter as you step toward its heart, lamplight reflecting off thickening layers of gold. Near the sanctum sanctorum, the home of this supreme lord, the line of pilgrims compresses itself into a denser body, hands raised high in supplication and bodies raised onto the tips of toes which inch forward up a ramp.

From the crest of the ramp comes the first sight of the Lord. The most excited of the men shout 'Govinda!', a version of their lord's name, and pump their clasped fists high in triumph. The god, heavy with ornaments and cloth of gold, looks out from his black face. He stands tall and a little distant, beyond the curve in the stream of adoring humanity, a real sense of power gathered in his stillness. The pilgrims approach the rail that keeps them from him, then walk backwards to keep him in their sights for as long as possible.

I made my passage before the Vishnu, but the outing was not yet complete. The doctor and I sat for a moment so that the grace of this encounter with God had time to settle within us, then joined the continuing line that passes around a cage that holds many men who squat on the floor sorting mountains of silver coins. This is the second wealthiest temple in India. To keep it so the pilgrim line winds itself around a cauldron bound in a cone of white cloth. People reach up to drop their own contributions inside.

Food is given to all who wish it. Priests sit and use a coconut shell to scoop out balls of rice and cashews encased in a banyan leaf. It is a present from the god. Lord Venkateswara is not a friend but he makes a good father figure, a power who chooses to dispense goodness and cares for all who come to him.

My journey still lacked its friend.

We climbed back onto the scooter and throbbed our way along the downward road that threads through these seven sacred hills, to hit once again the heat of the plain.

The scooter ride across the plain was like a journey into a convector heater, a passage through a wind of heat and grit. It eased at the edge of what seemed to be a fairground as the scooter slid into its slot and parked.

I headed for the first stall, a cool drinks stand, and poured liquid into my body. Now I was watered I was like a vine, newly energized, taking my sandals off to snake barefoot between the swarm and press of the crowd, heading for space where I could grow. I followed rough, hand-painted signs to an 'ashram', climbed a small flight of steps, and was granted admission to a hall where large fans churned some coolness into the air.

The hall was divided into two levels, so that the higher level appeared as a stage. An archway framed with banana leaves had been set up to the right of this stage, and below it a large group of ladies squeezed themselves one against the other. They lifted themselves onto their toes for extra height and extra thinness, so all could be as close as possible to this archway and have something of a view.

Suddenly a throng of people streamed in to fill the space behind them, and excitement rose in a clamour that drew back into a more respectful buzz then found its focus in the devotional chants of the women. I looked on from the back of the auditorium as a man in the orange robes of a Hindu monk stepped from behind a screen and onto the stage.

It was a simple entrance. Often spiritual performers inflate themselves before coming on stage, their legs like the trailing anchor of a balloon as the air that is in them propels them forward. Or they enter heavily, their stage appearance simply one more burden in life that they have to accept. Swamiji, for this was he, simply walked. While others on the stage danced and sprang about him, eager to find some way in which to serve, he strolled forward.

His hair and beard were black, full yet trimmed and neat. He displayed neither the ravaged austerity nor the ample plumpness I somehow expect of a monk, where the physical condition of life is either despised or wallowed in. He was simply a trim young man who seemed to be happy. He stood and smiled down at the women while they finished the song they had chosen for his arrival among them, then knelt down to accept the bolts of orange cloth they had brought as a present.

Then he stood, within his archway of banana leaves, and leaned out to look to his right. He lifted his hand to his chest, began to wave it, grinned, and mouthed a word.

"Hello".

I blinked back.

He mouthed "hello" again, and grinned more broadly at my confusion. This was a greeting just for me.

I grinned too, and raised my hand to wave my response.

The devotees climbed up to fill the stage, packing themselves around Swamiji. Then suddenly the sea of people parted. An avenue that broadened out toward me, and everyone's head turned in my direction. At the head of this avenue, sealing it since he was its destination, stood Swamiji. He held the index finger of his right hand in front of his face. It beckoned me toward his stillness.

I walked forward and introduced myself.

"Have you eaten?" Swamiji asked.

I had. My meal in the temple from Lord Venkateswara.

"No," I lied.

"Then you will eat with us. Afterwards we will talk."

I sat with the core of Swamiji's followers, those that were helping to organize this great day, on the floor of the room behind the meeting hall. Our plate-sized strips of banana leaf were placed before us on the ground, and a meal brought round.

Swamiji did not join us. This was a time for people to talk about his greatness, and their particular degree of closeness to him. They reminisced too about the great festival on the mountaintop the previous October. The occasion being celebrated beyond our walls was magnificent, some five thousand pilgrims a day being served with food for their bodies and food for their souls, but the previous Yaga was a miracle of the present age.

The meal complete, I moved to the stage in the meeting hall to await my call. I watched as many others, alone or in family groups, were ushered past the screen and into Swamiji's private quarters for their audience, and wondered when my call would come.

The sun dropped outside, though the night was lit by a kilometre or so of coloured bulbs that trimmed the canopy of the arena in the courtyard outside. The thousands sat on the ground, on the dust or on mats. The bullhorns of loudspeakers amplified the speech and music of the evening and charged it into the air above their heads.

Swamiji was the occasion's main speaker. The time in the schedule had come for him to lead some chanting. He could not speak to me now. I went and sat in the crowd to await his entrance on stage.

He walked onto the stage, as casually as if he were taking his seat in the audience, and sat down at its centre. He was carrying his emblem, a long wooden staff with a white cloth tied to the top. His entrance conjured no hush among the noisy crowd.

Swamiji had a following of young boys. A retinue of boy monks in their orange robes settled on the floor around him, and the chant of the sacred scripture started. His voice was clear, his memory good, the scripture long.

While he chanted, he spotted me in the audience, grinned, nodded his head, and gave me a little wave of his hand.

I returned to the hall. Many hours had now passed since the promise that we would talk. This was one of the busiest days of the Swamiji's life, but then a promise was a promise.

I asked some of the younger men how old Swamiji was.

"37," they said.

"Like me," I said. "Or nearly. I'm 38."

They were duly astonished. I was used to being taken for someone much younger than I am. It seemed it had happened again.

"So young," they said instead. "We thought you were much, much older than that. In your fifties. Look at your grey hair."

My call came. I was led behind the screen and into the first small room on the right. Swamiji was only visiting this temple. It was not his usual base. The room was small, its walls painted light blue, rattan matting on the floor, an air conditioner filling it with what passed for cool and so breathable air. Swamiji nodded and invited me to sit down. Did I mind if he carried on speaking with his visitors?

A steady flow of people brought their questions and devotion to him. As the room filled with one particularly extended family, I moved from the doorway to sit by his side.

Everyone that entered prostrated themselves as they came in, their chests and chins upon the ground, their hands extended toward him. No-one left the room without being given a gift, usually an orange, apple or banana drawn from a large supply at his side. They cupped their hands so the fruit could be dropped down and into their keeping. Tiny children were shown how not to reach out and take, but to wait and receive in this way. The moment came when Swamiji could turn his full attention to me. He asked me for a question.

We were in an area of sacred hills, and he had performed the age's most spectacular ceremony on top of the mightiest of them. So I formed my question around my quest.

"What can humans learn from seeing and visiting sacred mountains?" I asked.

He had been sitting with his legs curled round in front of him, one hand on the floor for support. Now he pulled himself erect and established himself in a full yogic posture. He was pleased with my question, and smiled as he began to answer it.

"Gods choose mountains and hillocks to stay on, and that is why we worship them," he said. "All over India there are hills with their local gods, and they are worshipped. But the question is, why do Gods choose hills? A light on the floor only gives light to those around it. On the plain a God would be the same, but from a hillock he can spread his influence to many people. And God is compassion. Compassion runs down the mountain to all who need it."

It was a kind answer, especially since few people would have attempted any answer at all. I thanked Swamiji, for his wisdom and welcome, and prepared to go. He looked around for something to give me. His stock of fruit was gone.

"Have we no books in English?" he asked his attendants.

There were none.

"I have a book," I said. It was a small book of the Swamiji's I had bought and read while waiting to see him.

"But that is a book for kids," he said.

"I am a kid," I replied and laughed as Swamiji laughed with me.

He gave me a bag filled with crystal sugar. Then someone found an old apple for him and he gave me that too.

"Sugar for sweetness, and an apple for life," he said as he handed them over and invited me to visit him any time.

I had found my friend.

When Guru Narayana had reached out of his mountain hut on Arunachala and given me some sugar, I was surrounded by monkeys. I was able to take one crystal of the sugar for myself, and set the rest on the ground. Monkeys swiftly scooped the offering into their mouths.

Now I was staying on the third floor of a large hotel near the bus station in town, with a bag of sugar I was not inclined to eat. I had seen no monkeys anywhere. A sow and her piglets were snuffling through a pile of garbage outside the hotel door, but feeding them did not seem an appropriate use of the gift.

I ate my apple, left my sugar in a glass on my dressing table, and wished there were a monkey to give it to.

I slept

A crash disturbed me in the night.

I woke the next morning to find the dressing table wet with urine. Two monkey turds had been deposited on my stool. Fair exchange was no robbery. The window was open, the glass was knocked over, and the sugar was gone.

~~~~~~~~~~

Swamiji was head of a venerable order, but a holy man from the religion of my birth also used to live nearby. One of the very earliest saints.

They called him 'Doubting Thomas' because he would not believe in the resurrected body of Jesus without pressing his fingers into the wounds of crucifixion. Others had the faith to believe on sight. Thomas was young. He needed to touch flesh.

I liked the boldness of Thomas's approach. Jesus bothered to appear in the flesh after all. It made sense to touch him. It makes sense to lay doubts to rest.

I was surprised to learn that St Thomas had moved from Jerusalem to live his life in Madras, and so I headed off to visit his Indian mountain home.
~~~~~~~~~~

5
St Thomas Mount Madras, India

Dimmer souls than Marco Polo waste words trying to dispel the beauty of myth. His travels were made up of them. Nowhere was too far to go to find a good story.

He came to Madras and heard from the locals that St Thomas had been there before him, and so he learned of the Apostle's last days on a hill some way inland from the city.

After a busy life treading the Indian coast and preaching the life of Christ, Thomas retired to a hilltop hermitage. As he sat, still and in prayer, peacocks gathered around him. They spread the thousand blue eyes of their tails to look down on him and bathe the saint in their shade.

A chink revealed itself in their surrounding cover, a gap not covered by the birds' bodies and tails, a gap no bigger than the wound pierced by a lance in the side of Christ. A man whom history records only as an idolater saw the peacocks, wanted their meat, and so set an arrow in his bow and let it fly. The arrow found the chink in the birds protection, flew through the flock so that not a feather was ruffled, and struck the saint in his side.

Thomas did not pause in his prayers. He diverted them to thanking the Lord for His mercies, and died.

Blood spurted from his wound and hit the cross before which he was praying. It was a cross he had carved himself from black stone, a bas-relief with words in the language of Nagari Paladu inscribed in an archway above it - 'Through the Cross-Suffering, the Messiah (Christ) brought salvation to the world'. Christians carried his body away for burial beneath the city's cathedral, and took pinches of the earth from where he fell. No matter how much earth they took away, its colour was always red.

Walls of rain walk about the earth. They are often to be seen far out at sea, or swamping distant mountains. God also draws them over the land of southern India at the end of each year, like sweeps of a curtain before the roar of a theatre's applause. Cyclones shove at their heels, but these walls of rain are too vast to be hurried.

The oilskin flaps of the autorickshaw were tied across the doors. Rain squirted in through the gaps, some of it brown from the road and some of it coming in just as rain. The highway had become a river. We pushed against the current like a tugboat, cradled between our own upsurging waves.

The rickshaw was halfway good. It had a windscreen but no wipers. The driver kept his handlebar at full throttle for the engine to spit out water and keep roaring. He leaned forward, to keep out of the rain coming in from the sides as much as in hope of seeing. The usual traffic had found anchor somewhere, so we had little to hit.

We looked for the tributary that would lead us left beyond the airport, and motored down it. The driver parked. It was time for me to get out and walk.

I untied the oilcloth. The rain faded. I stepped out onto ground that glistened with rain, and into air that was fragrant and dry.

All that one could hope for from a sacred hill.

An archway leads onto the 134 steps that climb the 300 feet of St Thomas Mount. Rain was bubbling down the steps as a waterfall. It is not a hard climb, but even so the hill is kindly and lets you take your time. Saplings were growing into a sacred grove halfway up, where pilgrims can rest a while.

Stations of the cross decorate the stairway, life-sized images from the Crucifixion story cast in black iron. The figures of the crucifixion on the summit are in white, Jesus staked to a red cross backed by a taller column of black and white checks. The black iron statues then resume to form a gentle curve around the hilltop to the pieta in a far corner.

The path passes between two buildings. One houses a crèche for abandoned children run by the convent of the sisters of the Franciscan missionaries of Mary. The other is a modest yellow-walled church built by the Portuguese in 1523.

Inside is the spot where St Thomas was martyred in 72 AD.

There are claims by scholars that the story of Thomas in India was manufactured by the Catholic Church, to establish the primacy of Christianity in the country and assert that the apostle was killed by a Hindu assassin. Such debate seems fitting for a saint who is famed for his own doubting.

The same scholars date the black cross, which St Thomas is said to have carved in the first years of our Lord, to the 8th Century. This cross is now the centre-piece of the altar. It was discovered in the 16th century, while the church was being built on the ruins of a Vishnu temple destroyed by the Portuguese. The stone stood for a while as though recovering, then sweated out its store of grief. Between 1551 and 1704, on the 18th December each year, it is recorded as oozing drops of blood.

Beneath the altar is a portrait of the Madonna and child, brought to India by Saint Thomas and attributed to Saint Luke. In its prefiguring of skills acquired in the Italian Renaissance, it is almost as much of a miracle as a bleeding cross.

The Apostle's body was carried down the hill to the beach, and then to the Cathedral of St Thomas in Madras where he is reputed to lie at rest. A scrap of him has been left behind though, a fragment from his bones. This relic is encased in glass and lodged at the centre of a silver crucifix.

After my passage through India and the rounds of Hindu Gods it was a great relief to be embraced by a culture that was my own. The statues of a man bearing a cross bigger than himself were episodes in a story I knew. The celebrations of a martyr's death; a painting of a mother and child from antiquity; an ancient stone carving that once wept blood; a scrap of yellow bone in an ornate silver symbol. It was all as strange as anything in a Hindu temple. I was simply spared the strain of understanding.

I lit a squat candle in an alcove to one side, as I knew how to do, and left it burning.

~~~~~~~~~
~~~~~~~~~

St Patrick climbed a mountain. So did Moses, Elijah, Mohammed, Jesus. Why not St Thomas too? Not this little mountain reserved for his old age, but a real one, a peak that rises through jungle and reaches high above the clouds.

Across the sea in Sri Lanka rises an almost unassailable peak. For years no path measured the final ascent. Pilgrims had to swing upwards from iron rings hammered into the bare rock face. Many spun in the wind and were hurled to their deaths, yet still they kept on coming.

They came because of the holy being who had come before them. This divinity impressed a footprint of vast proportions into the topmost rock.

Buddhists say it is the footprint of Buddha.

Moslems claim the footprint for Adam, the point where he touched Earth after being thrown from paradise.

Hindus claim it for Shiva, a step in the god's cosmic dance.

And a little band of Christians, God bless them for stretching their tremulous faith so far, claim this is the footprint of their very own Saint Thomas.

I set off to see for myself.

6
Adam's Peak
Sri Lanka

At each turning of the tide men stepped and then swam through the ocean, climbing poles from which they plucked fish from the water. Their coming and going marked the rhythm of my days. I swung in a hammock between coconut palms, read books or let them drop, and took time to recover. The shock of reaching Sri Lanka after India was the pleasant shock of the island's comparative lushness, its tidiness, its sense of order.

The sun rose, the sun set, late monsoon rains swept in and away, and my Sri Lankan life was life at its sweetest apart from flu and the prospect of facing another mountain. Adam's Peak seemed like a mountain out of fairy tales, and I had always been allowed to climb those in my imagination without having to go through physical hardship.

The game with Adam's Peak is to climb it at night. When you reach the summit before dawn your body will be tired but your soul will rejoice for a miracle of beauty is performed. The pyramid of the mountaintop is cast as a long shadow across the white bank of cloud far below, then as the sun climbs the mountain breathes the shadow back into itself.

It sounded beautiful. Having read the description I could imagine myself up there.

I waited till I had the stamina to sit on a bus then moved inland, across an astonishing range of tea plantations as the sequence of buses rose through mountain after mountain of tended bushes, and brought me to my destination of Ratnapura.

'Ratnapura' translates as 'Gem City'. A travelling salesman told me a joke on my first night in town.

Q: "Why do babies in Ratnapura clench their fists?"

A: "Because they're hiding a gem to sell to their mothers."

It is a gem town like I imagine a gold town to have been - shacks made permanent with cement to draw money from those that have made it, no-one really planning to stay here, just passing through on their way to making a mint.

The British came here. They erected a library with a sloping red pantiled roof, next to a clock tower built in remembrance of the victims of the Great War, then they too went on their way.

"You like gems?" men kept asking me.

"No."

"You want to see gem polishing?"

"Not at all."

They brought out white plastic jewel boxes with transparent lids, stones of reds and blues cut as diamonds or shaped like hearts, mine for a thousand rupees though not worth fifty. I would not keep them if they fell out of a Christmas cracker.

The town's Rest House is a vast colonial building, now government run. It has a verandah that stretches itself in front of a broad and glorious panorama of thickly-wooded hills, where one can sit in wicker-work chairs and take tea brought on trays by barefoot waiters. The same panorama could be enjoyed from my tiny bedroom. I sat and looked out at the treetops of the distant rainforest, and imagined myself to be a 19th century explorer in the grand British tradition.

My research into this latest mountain pilgrimage progressed by overhearing a conversation through my bedroom door. A German girl was telling how she had come with the thought of climbing Adam's Peak, but that it seemed impossible. This confirmed what I was learning. It was December 13th. The monsoon rains should have stopped, the pilgrimage season should have started, but I had got all my calculations wrong. The season didn't start until Poya day, December's full moon which would come on December 28th this year. Until then the path was unlit and the wildlife, weary of the monsoon rains, was ready to turn nasty. Elephants used the cleared paths to rest at night, and the tigers were hungry.

The stories of tigers I dismissed straight-out, knowing they were extinct on the island. 'Tigers' was just the wrong English translation for 'leopards'. I had last seen a leopard in a cage near Arunachala, slinking its body away from people's stares. I didn't particularly fear leopards. I trusted that they would much sooner run the wilds of a mountain than seek any human contact.

But the elephants? The temple elephant at the foot of Arunachala had trampled a lady to death and savaged her own keeper.

"Our elephants are small ones," laughed the man in the Rest House's gem shop, who courteously yet vainly tried to interest me in souvenirs.

A bus would take me round to the other side of the mountain, where I could start a much simpler, shorter and more popular choice of ascents. By coming to Ratnapura I had chosen the classic pilgrimage route, more awesomely long and up through jungle. It was these beasts of the jungle that threatened most danger, locals assure me. If I was to insist on the night-time jungle ascent, a reliable guide was essential.

I reported as much to Helga. Now the bedroom door was no longer between us she proved to be a willowy young German dental assistant of high cheekbones and lustrous tresses of light brown hair. I found myself excited by her company.

A silhouette of the mountain is the emblem on the town's buses, but otherwise Adam's Peak was not to be seen. I was directed to a few vantage points in town where I might have caught a glimpse, but the clouds were too low. I found a book about the pilgrimage tradition to the mountain instead, and carried it back to the Rest House. I was in no hurry. I could imagine this ascent for days more yet.

I sat in a wicker chair and a waiter padded his barefoot way upstairs with my tray of tea. Helga was behind him.

"Hello," she said. "I've found a guide. We're about to set off up the mountain. Do you want to come too?"

"Who is he?"

A good boy, I was assured. A friend of her friend's gem-dealing friend, a good Buddhist who had been helping her all morning. It was a toss-up between two forms of laziness. I could remain sitting, or I could save myself the bother of finding a guide of my own.

Lorna had conditioned me to climbing mountains on demand. The sun shone, then she would say it was a good day for mountains. Clouds rolled in, well then we might as well climb above them. You feel well, then let's go climb a mountain. You feel under the weather, well then let's walk it off. A gulp of mountain air never hurt anyone.

I gulped my tea, packed my bag, and went to join Helga and her young friend in the waiting car.

"Hello," the good Buddhist said. He had a glossy face, short hair curled in an attempt at dreadlocks, and excellent English learned during four and a half months with his Japanese girlfriend in Brighton. I had learned as much the previous evening when he tried to con me, leading me to the wrong guest house so he could grab his commission.

"Do you remember me?" he asked, then giggled and swigged from his bottle of arak, the local yellow spirit made from the nectar of the coconut flower.

The driver of the car took his arak in a glass. I had met him too. He had tried to sell me gems just one hour before.

I got out of the car.

"If he's coming, I'm not," I declared.

It was supposed to sound bold, but I expect it sounded petulant. I had barely met Helga, and already I was demanding she choose between me and another man. Her head turned between these men and me. She had trust to place in someone and had a choice of strangers.

Within an hour Helga and I were seated on a packed bus, at the start of a journey into the night. We had shed our common sense and given ourselves into the care of a wilderness, and each other.

"Is that Sri Pada?" I pointed, asking the young boy monk on the seat in front of me, choosing the local Buddhist name for the mountain out of deference to his tradition. The name translates as 'holy footprint'.

He smiled and shook his head, but I continued to believe. We had been an hour on the journey, dusk was settling in, and I was anxious to see my mountain before facing it in the dark. This choice of the peak that had come into view seemed quite suitable, detached from the span of mountains that reared to its right, its outline sharp against the sky, its sides sheer enough to make the ascent a worthy if perhaps impossible achievement.

We climbed from the bus and I set myself walking toward it.

"No," a local said. He laughed and turned me round toward a

path that led up through the village.

"Adam's Peak?" I checked.

It seemed unlikely. This mountain was sealed by clouds, which vouched for its height, but the shape was too broad, more like a wall, and I could not see how it would resolve itself into a sharp peak 7360 feet high.

"No, after. After."

The man's hand made a gesture of scooping back the clouds to show how our goal lay in some distant, high beyond.

I thanked him and he laughed again as he watched us on our way.

The main commerce of the village of Sri Pagama comes from the passing pilgrim trade, so it is better to have a house beside the route a steep mile's climb up the mountainside than one set ten yards back from its base.

The village is therefore very long.

The buildings start as shops before becoming houses, and at the junction between them is the temple dedicated to Saman, the Buddhist God of the mountain. It is Saman who legend tells whisked Buddha to the top of Adam's Peak where Buddha set down his footprint. On Saman's first pilgrimage to the footprint on the mountaintop he was met by a small white elephant, who presented him with a red lotus flower held within its trunk so that the proper floral offering could be made. Portraits now twin the god with the elephant, both happy with their blooms. This temple of Saman was our true point of departure. Some villagers gathered round to see us on our way, the young and the old and the curious, but the raucous clamour of goodbyes was not from them.

It was from a mass of dogs.

The loudest noise come from the ring of dogs that dashed forward yapping barks between backing off with growls. A tighter ring was dancing around my feet, lop-eared puppies seemingly of one brood though of a great genetic mix for they had all come out a different colour, from black through grey and brown to white. And near the heart of this circle was a white dog, little more than a puppy herself. She was whining with love. I don't know in which previous life we had met, but we had clearly been very close and this was a happy reunion. I bent down, a long way, to stroke my hand through the thick softness of her fur.

Loving though the dog was, she wasn't Miss Popularity about the place. As we walked up through the village she attempted to follow in my wake. This meant running the gauntlet of every neighbourhood dog. I warded them off with my flashlight as they skirled around each other and lunged for chunks from the little dog's flesh.

The distance between the houses and these onslaughts lengthened, and the dog began to gambol in front.

"They were her puppies," Helga noticed, and when I looked it was obvious the little white dog was carrying milk. "What will we do? Will she come with us?"

I thought about the puppies, thought about being concerned, but gave it up. You have to trust a mother's instincts. If the dog felt like climbing the mountain for a break, I was not going to kick her back downhill.

And besides, we were meant for each other.

On the slopes of a sacred mountain it was probably fair to be superstitious. I looked for such signs as this, something to show me that the odd course of my life was proceeding with a blessing. This little white mother dog fit the bill. I had been given my guide. She was a little like the canary carried by miners - when the canary snuffs it, retreat - but I reckoned she was there more out of friendship than sacrifice. Her colour showed up well in the flashlight as she led the way.

I turned the flashlight back on Helga.

"You've got one too," I told her.

A small brown dog had snuck in at her heels, camouflaged by his colour against the path. He was more pug-nosed, a bit of a bruiser, his body scabbed with the scars of several battles. Probably father to the mixed brood of puppies.

Our party was complete.

After leaving the last of the houses behind we met a man descending by the light of a flaming torch. He was shocked that we were going the other way.

"Elephants," he said, shaking his torch at the dark mountainside. "Tiger."

We smiled and nodded, and continued.

The fireflies here hung singly in the night. I was glad. A pair of them would have looked too much like a tiger's eyes.

Helga hoisted her bag onto her head and stepped like an old hand, fresh from a life walking the tea plantations.

"Have you climbed much?" I asked her. Part of me feared she would claim to be a world-class mountaineer. I doubted I was ready for another such woman. Another part of me hoped for the chance to surrender once again to a pair of competent hands.

"This is my first mountain," Helga replied.

I asked further questions. Lorna would have saved me the bother by pronouncing a catalogue of her phenomenal achievements at the first possibility. Helga simply waited and gave me her answers one by one. This was her first mountain. Her first night-time walk. Her first walk with dogs. Her first jungle. It began to seem that in the scale of her lifetime's adventuring achievements, our simple expedition was already near the top. The naivety of this expedition struck me as touching. Then it struck me as obvious. Naivety was essential to the night's quest. Anything more sensible would have got in the way. It would have commanded that we turn round and go back to civilization at once.

Lorna had a pet name for me. It came from an old Spike Jones record about a horse who was always last in the field. The horse's name was Beedlebum. Lorna would stand on rocks, cast her mane of hair into the wind, and call the name down at me to coax me higher and faster. Come along, Beedlebum. You can do it, Beedlebum. If I was Beedlebum still, Helga had backed me. She had staked all her money on my crossing the line. Somehow it made a difference as I led the way up the track.

The path was steep, an arduous round of lifting one foot above the other and heaving ourselves behind. Times I heard myself laughing, a short laugh (a braying laugh, Lorna might have said) that served as a catch of breath. I was still detached enough from the strain of the walk to find the thought of what we were doing fun.

The lighting was not yet turned on for the season but the lamp-posts and lamps, minus their bulbs, stood like public showers along the way to confirm we were on course. The refreshment stations were there too, some standing as roofless skeletons of themselves but others intact and offering good shelter though no food or drink. We floated around them like ghosts among ruins.

Helga seemed ready to turn the first one into our home. It consisted of a roof supported on thin wooden pillars. Helga pulled a very long sheet of purple plastic out of her bag and spread it across a high bench.

"We'll stay here?" she both asked and decided in the very same moment. Lightning filled the sky behind us. "It will rain soon. We will sleep here, then carry on."

Her assurance beguiled me, as assurance often does. I pulled off my tee-shirt, wet with sweat. I had learned from books of jungle exploration to stay warm in this way, putting the wet clothes back on before resuming the trek. Helga copied me. For a moment, semi-naked in the paleness of our flesh, Helga's tender breasts turned a night-time alabaster by the phosphorous light of the forest, we were ghosts indeed. Side by side we sat on the plastic sheet, ate a banana from our meagre store of food, and shared a couple of biscuits Helga had bought at a baker's in town. They had come highly recommended by the baker and were a prophetic choice in the light of our new companions. They were as crunchy as dog biscuits with something of the same taste, and threatened to crack even the two dogs' jaws.

Five minutes passed.

"Right," Helga decided. "There is no rain after all. Shall we go on?"

I pulled on my wet tee-shirt, and led the way at her command.

We had heard about a watchman who lived halfway up the mountain, and saw a light ahead. It was the first of several lamps lit between a run of empty buildings; one was a large shed that would serve well as a dormitory, and the others would become shops or restaurants, but right now the tourist complex was off-season with a vengeance.

Most of the light was gathered around the final building on the left, a small mud-walled house with a tin roof. Two men came out onto its verandah and invited us inside. We stepped through their door and into still more light. A bar of an electric fire glowed red, and a kettle was plugged in to boil away.

The men were from the electrical company and had connected themselves to the supply. These electricians had come up the mountain on November 1st to prepare the way for the pilgrimage season, and would stay until it closed at the end of May. In the six weeks they had been here, the older man with good English said, there had been three other pilgrims on the route.

"We are numbers four and five?" Helga asked, hardly believing the answer. She had been expecting a large company of fellow souls to walk with.

The man nodded. He had already told us we should walk no further, that beyond this point was the jungle of tigers and elephants. If we had chosen the short route up the other side we would have been alright, but no-one should walk through the unlit jungle at night.

"How far to the next place where we could sleep?" Helga asked.

"Two and a half hours. Three hours to the top."

We had been told the walk would take us four hours in all. We had come almost two, so had presumed we were halfway. It seemed as well to sleep here.

Right where we were seemed wonderfully suitable. We were seated on a comfy bed, bright with a red checked woollen blanket. Perhaps the men would have let Helga stay, but I wasn't prepared to leave her on her own. Gamely I stood up to lead the way outside. The dogs and Helga followed.

We were shown to a large bare hall opposite, and a bench big enough for two if I tucked in my legs. Helga spread her plastic sheet, we switched out of our tee-shirts again, and her preparations continued. Her bag seemed to yield everything -- a mattress, a pillow, a couple of blankets. In a few minutes she was stretched out and snug.

"You told me you could never sleep when travelling," I reminded her.

"This isn't travelling," she said. "I'm with you. I feel safe. Goodnight."

I tucked the tee-shirt under my end of the plastic as a pillow, wrapped my arms around my chest for warmth, and looked out to the open far-end of the hall where the sky flashed light blue. White dog curled herself on the floor beneath me, while brown dog prowled a little. Sounds studded the darkness - the obvious crickets, but clucks and tappings and whoops and cries I could not fix to any animal. Behind them all was the softer sound of Helga's sleeping breath.

I did sleep, or a curious comfortable mixture as though my body was slung between dreaming and waking. At 2.30 I stood up.

"Shall we go?" Helga sat up and suggested.

"OK."

"In thirty minutes. First I will eat."

We breakfasted on banana and biscuit, put on our wet clothes, and slithered up the next run of steps.

We now had to go fast in our bid for the sunrise, that moment that strikes those who see it with a sense of supernatural beauty, the shadow of the summit projecting itself onto the clouds below then being absorbed back into the mountain.

"Please stop," Helga asked. "Can you give me light?"

She rolled up her trousers. Short brown worms were clinging to her legs, swiftly growing fatter. I watched, and offer the translation for her German *Blutedeln*. They were leeches.

Ibn Battuta wrote of these creatures in his twelfth century journal:

"In this place we saw the flying leech, which sits on trees and in the vegetation near water. When a man approaches it jumps out at him, and wheresoever it alights on his body the blood flows freely. The inhabitants keep a lemon in readiness for it; they squeeze this over it and it falls off them."

I had heard of neither the leeches nor the lemon juice. Helga was actually carrying a small bottle of lemon juice in her bag, and had smoothed it into her arms and face to keep insects at bay. Piercing the night with her pencil torch, hers was the perfect minimalist packing, a fullness of emergency supply that would have left even Lorna satisfied, if only we had known how to make full use of it.

It was a minute or so before it occurred to me to check myself. I started by trying to roll back my right sock. It was stuck to my leg with blood. The leeches were hard at work all over me. I pulled them off and their bodies twisted round to suck at my fingers, still clinging as I tried to shake and flick them off.

This was our only real break as we chased up through the last of the night, enjoying a piece of open ground where the path crossed large rounded boulders, mourning the loss of height as we followed the route down a dip, searching the path with flashlight up to the next bend to check for any resting hulks of elephants. We raced and raced till the darkness faded and it was useless racing any more. Our dawn would not be on the summit. It was to be no more than an ordinary miracle, when the foliage turns green and the world becomes visible.

Then, for the first time, we saw our goal.

It looked a little silly, as though it weren't part of our mountain climb at all. Our mountain was solid, broad and mighty. This peak looked manufactured, as though when the Earth was still molten God had taken a pinch of it and pulled it high. Covering its pinnacle was the trim roof of a small temple.

I had so wished to be up there at first light, but it was still quite clearly hours of walking ahead of us. We reached a bridge that crossed a river, walked down to the boulders in the water, and scooped handfuls into our mouths.

"We are so lucky," Helga said, "to be here at dawn."

Darkness peeled away to reveal the dawn. Helga saw this first, then I noticed it too. She had started with no goal, no image of the peak's shadow on clouds below, and was now in love with the apparition she had been given. She had passed through the night and emerged in a tropical mountain stream. Her new day shimmered with wonder.

When I stopped wishing I was somewhere else, I learned to see through her eyes. It was beautiful to be able to see just where we were.

We settled in the beauty for a while.

A silver-painted triumphal archway spanned the path for us to pass through. A small Buddha lodged in a shrine at the foot of the final ascent. I could see the logic in Buddhists pausing here to send up a few prayers. The last of our climb looked awesome.

The summit of Adam's Peak resembles the rock that is topped by a castle in the Disney logo, the magic kingdom revealed in fairy tales when you emerge from a forest. Unlike Disneyland, the place lacks a cablecar. The approach is a treadmill of high concrete steps. I used both hands to haul myself up the handrail, and stopped for a rest at the goal of every lamppost.

With the dawn Helga had grown extra sprightly, and seemed set for sprinting. I caught sight of her up ahead sometimes, the dogs keeping pace with her. She waited for me near the top. I had saved the boon of her journey till this moment, when she might be most glad of it.

"Here's the good news," I told her, when the pain in my lungs subsided enough for me to speak. It was a piece of information I had read in an account of the mountain. "As a woman who has completed the classic route up this side of the mountain, rather than the feeble climb up the other side, you will be born as a man in your next life."

"Is that good?" she asked.

At least she didn't laugh at me, as Lorna would have done. Her smile perhaps allowed me some pity. Then she spurted out of sight up the final twists of stairs.

The mountaintop is tiered with white concrete steps, and crowded with white buildings. A police station and post office are in the outer ring, then steps through a wall lead up to the open pagoda built over the sacred footprint. This pagoda is mounted on a large lump of rock that looks like a separate import to the scene, but is really the summit peaking through the clutter. The images of Buddha and Saman had not yet arrived. Nor had the bell which pilgrims ring, once for each ascent they have made. Out of season these are stored in a temple far below. The air was charged with the smell of paint as three men with broad brushes rendered everything with a coat of silver.

I went in search of the footprint, ready to make my up own mind about which divine personality had left it. I made up a rhyme to help me decide:

"Buddha, Adam, St Thomas or Shiva

Which one convinces this believer?"

The footprint was housed under a roof in an open shrine. I sank to my knees before it.

In belief?

No. In disbelief.

There was nothing to see. Nothing at all. Not a toe, not a heel, not a trace remained in view. I later learned that so many pilgrims had been rubbing their foreheads across the faint image and wearing it away, the government had recently taken an enlightened decision to protect it. They had covered it in concrete.

Some coins lay on the ridged square of this concrete bed. Helga dropped one there too. I contented myself with the ritual of stepping over the bed, and away.

They say that heaven is forty miles from the summit of Adam's Peak. If so, it finds its reflection in the landscape that lay below us.

A broad sheet of cotton cloud spread wide and far to cover the sea and disappear into mist and a distant sky. This soft white canopy was pierced with the high green peaks we had passed on our walk, a green so dark and rich that I trembled for all that lay hidden below.

Helga sat herself on the other side of the summit, for here the sky was clear, and she gazed down at her own version of heaven. Far below the sun was shining on a tempered agricultural landscape patterned as fields. It brought a blue to the extensive splash of a lake. Helga was happy. She spoke to a workman and learned of a bus that headed back to town from this side. This descent would take an hour and a half instead of the seven hours of our route up, and I knew she would take it. The view down that side was so neat, so relatively mild, so much akin to her native Lake Konstanz that it had to draw her near.

The workman offered us dinner. We followed him to sit on the floor of a newly plastered large bare chamber. This was where the monks would sleep in season, and for now it was the accommodation and cooking centre for the workmen. Cold rice was prised from a bucket onto plastic plates and dribbled with dhal while our dogs were kicked out of the room. We ate a little, glad of food of any sort, and dropped wedges of rice into a plastic bag when no-one was looking.

Helga dipped in to her bag of the world's goodies to return the workman's gesture of kindness. Demonstrating how to make a roll-up cigarette, she left him with a selection of papers and a small pouch of tobacco.

It was time to head down the mountain. I looked down at the short and sunny route and imagined the scene. We would run down together, a Hansel and Gretel fresh from the forest, our little dogs skipping at our heels. Then we would jump on a bus and wave our dogs goodbye. "Home, dogs, home!" we would say. "Up over that mountain and down the other side. Watch out for leopards and be careful you don't get lost."

Helga recognized the dangers.

"We could throw stones at them," she suggested. "Make them leave us. They would go back on their own, and you could come down the short way with me."

This was a show of what I took to be female logic. It combined cruelty and kindness, without threatening her own preferred position. Whatever the decision, Helga would get her own way. She would go the short way, with or without me.

I could have admitted that I was too soft to throw stones at the dogs, but then she would have thrown them for me. Instead I volunteered to lead the dogs down through the jungle on my own, so we could be sure of their safety. If the solo jungle journey was bold it was also timid. Sustaining Helga's company seemed more fearsome in some ways. It would be verging on commitment.

We hugged our farewells and put on our socks and shoes. White dog showed no hesitation and came with me. Brown dog started off, but his loyalty was divided. He paused and looked back to where Helga had already disappeared.

I poured my bag of the workman's rice onto one of the steps.

Brown dog was convinced.

The security guard for the mountain came up the track on his daily round. He confirmed the reports of elephants and 'tigers', though he had not seen any that day. He had seen the dogs before though. They were the temple dogs, from the temple of Saman in the village below.

I was content to have been spared the Buddhist ritual of the route. Buddhists wind a white cloth around their heads, bathe in the sacred places, and place a stone on a cairn at their first sight of the peak. I was sure it was beautiful and of supreme importance to the devout, but it was pleasant not to have to pretend to be Buddhist. Adam's Peak is in an area of Sri Lanka deemed to be safe from terrorist or military attack. Further north the country was a no-go area, commanded by the Tamil Tigers who fight for a degree of separatism for their people. The mountain, like the island, is more than simply Buddhist.

But I was happy the Buddhist Lord of the Mountain had allowed us the company of his dogs as our guides.

Wildlife came at me with a sequence of calls from trees to either side, loud and shrieking caws from a body too large for a bird's.

White dog poised, alerted her floppy ears, and was off, chasing through the forest as a large monkey crashed and leapt between the branches above her head. It was a bear monkey, its dark purple face peering out through a bushy white beard. It bounded onto a branch and looked down at me, but I was too tired to stop and chat.

Three electricians were now inside their wayside home, and they invited me in for a hot milk drink.

"The lady. Where is the lady?"

I told them the story of Helga's descent down the other side.

"The lady?" they asked again, deaf with disappointment at only seeing me. "Where is she?"

A team of workmen passed me by, their tools hooked over their shoulders, skipping down the mountainside as blithely as the Seven Dwarves. The first large raindrops fell and they put up large brollies, while disappearing at a canter.

A door was laid like a platform under the eaves of one of the first houses in the village. A young man and woman sat on it and swung their feet, gazing out into the rain, as their infant daughter sheltered between them. They shifted up to leave me space to sit alongside, and the wife fetched me a drink of hot milk.

I rolled up my trousers and pulled off more leeches, then hopped across to an outside tap to wash my leg and rinse out my sock. Wring after wring washed blood into the channels of rain that raced down the path, and coloured them red.

Brown and white dogs hid themselves beneath me under the

door, guarded by my dangling feet, but as the rains grew I was asked indoors and the dogs were shooed away. I watched white one pad through the rain and round the corner. I had my warm milk, she had hers still to give. As I settled on a chair inside, brown dog managed to find his way in and sit beneath me once again.

"Buses to Ratnapura are very busy," the lady said. "No more buses. In this rain, no buses. My husband give you a lift. On his bike."

The motorbike shared this front room. Such passenger service was maybe their main form of business.

There would be buses. We both knew it. They had to spin their story, and I could choose whether to believe them or not. I thanked them for the kindness of their shelter and drink, and said goodbye.

"God bless," said the lady.

"And you," I replied, and a jolt of some truth in the blessing passed between us. We stared into each other's eyes, amazed by the power of the moment, before moving apart.

The puppies were frolicking about their little white mother on the temple verandah. She spotted me and left them trailing to come whimpering her love and greeting. The villagers in the street laughed to have her disappearance and reappearance explained. I took out two biscuits to say goodbye.

Goodbyes are not quite as simple as that. Brown dog trailed me all the way to the junction where I waited for the bus.

In every encounter there is a moment for a happy goodbye. Only one such moment. Beyond it lies attachment, and before it lies abandonment. The success of an active rather than a contemplative life comes from recognizing and responding to such moments of happy goodbye.

The last of my biscuits from Helga's store was ready. I flung it as I heaved myself aboard the bus with all the other passengers. It cracked loud in brown dog's jaws as we moved away.

Back in the Guest House my calves seized up when I tried to mount the stairs. I held on to the rail and walked backwards to get to my room. For days to come I would have to walk backwards when faced with any slope.

Helga reappeared eleven hours after our parting on the summit. She knocked on my bedroom door which had a latch and no bolt, and walked in.

"I am so late," she said. "The hotel wanted to sell me a room for the night but I said no, I will stay with you. They said you have a single bed only. I told them I have a mattress. I can sleep on the floor. In the morning, very early, my bus will leave. It is silly to spend money for just a few hours."

She turned the light on. The bulb was very low wattage and let out a dim light.

"You look sweet," she said. "You were dreaming?"

She did not wait for an answer but settled her two bags into a corner of the room and sat on the edge of my bed.

"The dogs were safe?" she asked.

"Yes," I said, sitting up.

"That's good. You are a good man." She reached across me to turn off the light, then pulled her tee-shirt over her head. The shutters were open to reveal her alabaster skin. "My way was fun. I found a waterfall and stripped off for a shower. It was wonderful. The power of water fell on my head and hit the rocks like thunder. I met lots of workers repairing the steps, and the path was sunny. It was lined with flowers. I could smell them as I walked by. Then I walked down through terraces of tea bushes, one after the other. Ladies in bright dresses filled their baskets with leaves. Then the bus. Hour after hour on the bus. It was a good day, Martin. A very good day. Now I am tired. We sleep, yes?"

She pulled off the rest of her clothes and lay them on her baggage, then climbed into my bed. I shifted aside to make room.

"You are like me," she said. "You sleep naked."

She slid her hands around my body.

"I'm tired," I said.

"Me too. And stiff." She reached between my legs. "Very stiff."

It took me back to student days, when love was squeezed into single beds. Helga's next words were in German, but in a dialect I did not understand. And then we slept, our bodies rolled into the single dent in the mattress.

"Are you going?" I asked, for she had slid from the bed and was putting on her clothes.

"It is time."

I turned on the dim light.

"It's not even dawn. Do you have to go?"

"My flight is booked."

"I'll come with you," I said and sat up.

"No." She spoke the word softly.

"I haven't got your address."

"No," she said again. "That's true. But there's no point. I'll be moving when I get back in any case."

She was now dressed. She carried her bags into the corridor then came back to stand above me.

"We were good together," she said. "A present for each other from the mountain. Now we move on."

She kissed me on the forehead, and was gone. The latch clicked into place on my door.

~~~~~~~~~~

I felt my mountain journey was complete, but that's the thing with mountains. You reach what you think to be the top, only to find another summit ranges above you.

I went to Germany, though not consciously in search of Helga. I was not consciously in search of sacred mountains either, though a small one was central to the place.

This German mountain, in the Westerwald region of Germany some way east of Cologne, attracted all sorts. Gnomes, elves and fairies were caught inside the bark of its trees, squeaking to be freed. I never saw them myself, but once walked the mountain's paths with a visionary Yorkshirewoman who kept pausing to beam telepathic advice into this fairyland. She claimed to be freeing sprites from the
~~~~~~~~~~

capture of trees and showing lost goblins the best way home. At the top of the small mountain, outside the walls of its ancient church, she watched tubes of blue light drop from heaven and hover a few feet above the ground.

Stations of the Cross are set beside the main path, statues telling the story of Jesus's climb up Calvary, but this mountain is no more Roman Catholic than Jesus was. A tumble of stones on one of its sides marks an ancient altar to the pagan god Wotan, yet Wotan has lost his currency and the mountain remains. The mountain is called Blasiussberg, and its slopes drop down to a village nestled in the valley below.

Our religions accept messages from mountains. Moses was led up Mount Sinai, Jesus was transfigured on the summit of Mount Tabor, Mohammed received the first recitation of the Koran in a mountain cave, Saint Patrick cast out Ireland's demons from the summit of Croagh Patrick, Padmasambhava relayed the secret powers of the Himalayas through Tibetan Buddhism, and a mountain revealed the Mormon scriptures to Joseph Smith. Mountains disseminate power through the actions of prophets and so affect our lives. It's a supreme comedy of the human condition that we pick up faint resonances from these mountains and call the experience God. We know things to the limits of our perception of them. Mountains bulk vast on our horizons yet we hardly know and respect them at all.

Our prophets can often be found on the flank of a mountain. The mountain need not be big, and indeed Blasiussberg is an easy trot up and down. A sacred mountain may even be a hill, but it will dominate the landscape around it. This is a book about love and sex and sacred mountains. I had not come to Germany for this mountain, for as with love and sex the power of sacred mountains was still a bit beyond my ken. I had come for the holy woman who had settled in the valley below. Word was whispering round that she was God on Earth in female form. It was Friday night, and she was about to open her home to visitors.

7
The White Cliffs of England

A young man dressed in white shirt, white trousers and white socks sat on the edge of the goddess's German porch.

"Do you speak English?" I asked.

His legs were drawn up and his hands draped loose around them. His hair was thin dark curls, his skin the white of duck eggs. He looked up, smiled slightly, spoke softly.

"I am English," he said.

I sat down to join him. James stood at the edge of the courtyard and watched. It had been love at first sight. Then I came along. The being that graced the porch was the angel of his fantasies. The ease with which I had insinuated myself next to his new love's side marked me as a loathsome smooth operator.

The doors of the house opened. Leaving our shoes on racks, we padded across the marble floor inside. The first concern was the etiquette of meeting a woman known as God. A page of instructions was set on chairs for newcomers. We were to keep silent throughout the evening. Rising to our feet both when the woman entered and left the room, we were otherwise to stay seated until we sensed our turn had come. Then we should move to a pine chair near the armchair where she would settle herself. The person before us would be kneeling at her feet. When they moved, we should take our turn to kneel in front of her while she placed her hands on our heads. When she removed her hands we were to look up into her eyes. She would then close her eyes, which was our signal to return to our seats and await the end of the evening.

So much, so simple. But when someone so lowly as a born-again preacher lays his hand on a supplicant's forehead, the person will swoon into the arms of fellow believers. Or maybe they'll lie quivering on the floor, speaking in tongues. If this woman was indeed God on Earth, such histrionics must seem banal compared to the effects she must have on her followers.

The village clock struck seven. A rustle of silk signalled the approach of two women into the hallway outside. The first was the woman's personal assistant. The second was the woman herself.

She was young. Her skin was dark, for she was born into a peasant family in rural India. Soft down covered her lower lip, for she was careless of beauty in its western format. Her entrance was a retreat from majesty, a softshoe shuffle across the floor. She was short, her head was bowed, and she made her way direct to her armchair where she settled down.

Her name, Mother Meera, was said to have been given her by the Goddess Durga. As God she was beyond restrictions of religion, though the red spot of Hindu devotion marked her forehead. Her hands reached out of her sari's purple silk and touched the head of her assistant. For some Mother Meera might burst into apparitions at this point. They might see her as the Indian Goddesses Durga, Parvati or Kali, as the Virgin Mary, as the Buddha. I was new to the game, so only saw a young Indian woman.

My turn came.

Jesus Christ gave us the model of God in the figure of a man. Here God in the figure of a woman was on offer. In coming to her home I had accepted that possibility. It's foolish to resent bowing down before God. My only concern was lack of practice. I wished to bow down with a natural elegance rather than passionate abandon. Where should I lay my hands? Should I wear my glasses?

As I sat on the pine chair and waited, I simply wished to stay alive. My heartbeats flared into savagery. Each one pounded like the strike of a heart attack. The next minutes were ones of survival as Mother Meera's head pulsed backwards and forwards, engaged in some transaction of energy with the person in front of her. I dropped to the floor the moment the space was clear and closed my eyes. Light fingers lay hold of the sides of my scalp, some pressure lightly pressed into place. Then the hands were removed. I sat up and gazed back into her eyes.

The eyes were large, with a great depth of brown. The shock to my heart had been enough. I saw nothing more sensitive in them than a sense of play. Her eyelashes dropped down to close her eyes from view, and I returned to my seat.

"Aren't we lucky?" the young Englishman said as we took the country lane up to our boarding house. "So very lucky, to be devotees of the divine mother."

I smiled in the face of such silliness. The evening had given me no proof of witnessing a divine mother, whatever such a being was. The thought of one visit turning us into devotees was absurd. I personally never intended to lose my mind in such a way, though of course I later did.

Some way behind, James watched my shadow slide along beside the white and willowy figure of his new love.

James Thornton was a serious figure. For years he had been a student of the Japanese Zen master Taezan Maezumi Roshi in Los Angeles. Basing himself at the Zen Center in LA he had founded an office of the National Resources Defense Council, a summit of years as one of the nation's foremost environmental lawyers. From a self-imposed retreat he had conceived a policy of environmental protection, based on preserving the habitat of a little bird called a gnat catcher, which has preserved many thousands of acres of Southern Californian coastline. Now he had set that work aside for a period of spiritual quest.

I had come to Germany on my way back from setting up a language school in Bangkok. James was heading for Nepal and a year's retreat with the Tibetan Buddhist master Sogyal Rinpoche. His light reading over the breakfast table was a large blue religious tome he had brought back from a recent pilgrimage to Tibet.

This is how I first noticed him. The boarding house was filled with people who had come to visit Mother Meera. They were full of the visit the following morning, chattering away over what had brought them there. Only James was apart. Dressed in a dark blue shirt, his curls trimmed close to his head, he had chosen a table in the annex. His plate of bread and cheese was cut into delicate slices, his pot of tea was poured, and he peered through his glasses into the pages of his spiritual text. He looked up occasionally, but more to quell our noise than out of curiosity.

I shifted the conversation on my table into literary discussion. James looked up. Though buried in a book, he didn't miss a thing. People's chatter about their lives was an inane chorus that smudged the beauty of silence. Talk about books was possible fun. He looked up again. I caught his eye.

"Why not join us?" I said.

He closed his book and brought it first to the table, then returned to fetch his food and drink. His solo breakfast spread was now constrained within our available slot. I liked to think I had brought him out of himself. More likely he had stepped across to come to know his enemy. I had moved in on the young man he loved. Perhaps I could let him in on some secrets. Perhaps I could introduce them, for indeed the young man was at my table.

The conversation resumed. Someone spoke of the stories of John Cheever. I mentioned the recent news that had come out of the writer's homosexuality.

"Is that so?" James asked. He lifted his head, sat more erect, and showed a spark in his eyes. "Then that makes his writing *much* more interesting to me!"

We walked and talked through much of the morning. James told ribald stories about St Thomas Aquinas, and exploded into a series of vivid impressions of Samuel Johnson. We both laughed a good deal. "You're a writer," I told him. "Even if you don't know it."

He was happy now. The young Englishman was staying, and I was leaving. My room was booked by someone else and the boarding house was full. We said goodbye.

James was bolder that evening. He was already seated on the porch of Mother Meera's house when the young Englishman arrived. He smiled, and the smile flickered away in surprise. I was there too.

"I thought you'd gone," James said.

"I've got a big room," the Englishman said. "With twin beds. He's staying the night with me."

James glared at me. "That's nice," he said.

That night, James lay awake in his single room, filled with dark imaginings of what the two of us were up to. The Englishman did keep me awake into the early hours. He told of his love for a French girl. They loved holding each other naked for hours and licking icecream off each other's spoons. His stories were as erotic as the adventures of Hansel and Gretel, but without the power of the witch.

In the morning we all got up early. James and the Englishman stood side by side in the doorway, waving me on my way.

For a year I kept returning to Germany to spend time with Mother Meera. James was always there. He had cancelled his pilgrimage to

Tibet and focused on a period of silent retreat, punctured by walks in the countryside and attendance at Mother Meera's thrice weekly open evenings. Each time I saw him an extra layer of reserve had been stripped from his face. His body was thin and his eyes were shiny.

He stepped out of solitude to walk the countryside with me. Blasiussberg was a favourite destination. Walking a path along its flank one day he went silent. I looked at him and found he was blushing. "May I ask you something, Martin?" he said.

Oh God, I thought, here it comes. He wants me to sleep with him. "A friend has sent me a manuscript of a novel for comment," he said. "You're a novelist. Would you mind reading it for him?"

Gladly! The embarrassment of rejecting my friend was avoided. The most I felt able to offer him in any physical way happened as we stood by the font on a visit to Limburg Cathedral. One of the curious facets of my early time with Mother Meera was an infusion of energy that came in through the crown of my head. It directed me to do what my upbringing would otherwise have rejected. It was very insistent, and since I felt it to be a loving force I obeyed it in the end. Standing by the font I got the inner command; "Hug this man!" I refused, and the flow of energy persisted. I flapped my arms around him and squeezed.

James moved from his guest house into one of Mother Meera's homes. After fourteen months he decided it was time to return to America and continue his environmental work. I followed the inner prompting once more, bought twenty red roses in the local florists, and walked them down to his front door. They would perfume his last days in residence. On my next visit he would be gone.

I found myself a teaching job and moved into a house on the southern English coast. It was in a hamlet called Birling Gap in the county of Sussex.

"And does it birl?" a Scottish friend asked me. 'Birl', she explained, is a Scottish word for 'blow'. The name made sense. Frequent winds rushed in across the English Channel, driving rains that heaved themselves against the cliffs. The cliffs are white and made of chalk, so often crack and fall into the sea. My house was one of a short string of coastguard cottages, the far end of which had already tumbled over the edge.

I moved in under cover of the darkness of New Year's Eve, and squelched through floods on the ground floor. The winds drove rain through every crack in the windows and door. When especially fierce they filled the sky with sea foam and painted the landscape white as though with winter snows. The back garden formed the beginning of a hill which rises as one of the Seven Sisters, a series of white cliffs that undulate as the coastline. The winds were so strong that at times it was possible to jump and fly a little way as I climbed the hill, or to lean back and accept the wind as my support.

James arrived in England on a visit. It was spring, and the weather was fair. We climbed the path that led up the hill from my door, carrying a flask of tea and box of cakes. With feet dangling over the cliff edge and staring out to sea we drank our tea, spoke about our favourite books, then stood to go back to my house. First though I wanted to examine a sheet of transparent plastic that was fixed to the ground some feet beyond our chosen spot.

It was the wrapping for a bouquet of flowers. A message attached to it read 'For our darling Sheila, who left this life from this place.' It was signed with love from her family.

I had seen this girl's face in 'Missing' posters. These cliffs are notorious for suicides. I thought of her family, making this climb and throwing their flowers off the cliff to follow her, and remained in silence for some time. Some force moved through me, as though I were a filter for a sorrow that clung to this place.

My house was rented. It was a place of single beds though I had a futon in the front room to pull out for guests. We pulled it out to prepare it so I could settle James in for the night. The day outside had been sunny but this was one of the wild spots on earth. Lightning flashed through the darkness outside, and with no seconds for counting thunder crashed against the sky. The whole house shook. We looked out as the storm hurled rain against the windows, looked at each other, and laughed the shock out of our bodies.

The flow of energy entered my head in the way it had done in Limburg Cathedral. "Hug this man" it said.

We held each other up against the storm for a while, then took shelter under the covers of the futon.

Some weeks later I returned to sit on the spot on the cliffs where James and I first drank tea. I faced the sun as it dropped above the sea. A seagull wound a constant circle of flight above me, shrieking with each circuit and dipping its flight toward my head. I looked over the cliff edge to check for any nesting young it might be protecting, but there were none. It seemed wrong to go away. I sat still for twenty minutes and tried to bless the bird, to calm it. Slowly the bird's circles of flight moved higher.

My culture is cynical about mystical moments. Expressing them leaves one open to charges of lunacy. When the world opens up in such a way the best you can do is give them your own quiet attention and see what unfolds. For me the pattern of having to accept the undeniable began as a teenager. Appropriately enough, it happened on a mountainside.

I had been told of a monastery in the Peloponnese that was a cool place to stay. It took a while to obtain clear directions in the nearest town. By the time we reached its outer walls night had already fallen. It turned out the monastery was in fact a convent, and its gates were closed for the night.

A nun sang a lullaby through an invisible window as my friend and I lay our sleeping bags on the ground. Soon we were asleep. Twice in the night my shoulder was gripped as though by a firm hand and I was shaken awake. Each time I looked across to where my friend was sleeping, and no-one else was around.

At the same time in London my sister was on an operating table, a delicate operation to save her from paralysis that had started in her face. The night before, in a youth hostel in Corinth, I had seen her in a dream. Her face was bloated and she was looking out at me as she stood in her hospital gown.

My sister, as she lay still before the surgeon, came to a distant mountainside to shake me in her need.

A need trembled around a world and a mountain stirred in sympathy.

So what's with the seagull?

I knew, in the way that fancies sometimes grip hold of your spine and send tears shooting out of your eyes, that the crying swooping bird was linked to the young woman who had jumped to her death from this place just weeks before. It was as though her spirit possessed the gull and sent it skirling round and round. She had jumped, but she had not broken free from the horror that had driven her over the cliff edge. Her spirit could fly, but it did not know how to fly free.

The night of the seagull's swooping a rash developed on my torso and neck. The splotches were large, as dense as chicken pox. I visited a doctor. She examined me. Though the rash was not contagious she advised me to stay off work till it subsided, for no-one would feel easy about working alongside me. She had seen nothing like it before, and could give me no idea what might have caused it.

I told the story to a friend in New York the following Christmas. Tears fell from my eyes in the telling. I have since learned how the dead can miss the ability to cry out the grief of what they have lost, and welcome the chance to let loose their tears through others. My friend, who was both a writer and editor, reached across the restaurant table and took hold of my hand.

"You must put this story in your book of mountains," she said.

"But it didn't happen on a mountain. It was a range of undulating downland that gets cut off by the sea. Part of a range of hills called the Seven Sisters."

"Honey," she said, and gave my hand a squeeze. "You're English. You just don't get it. Listen to your Aunt Babs. Take advice. Seagulls swooping in with the spirit of a dead girl is a great story. Include it. It happened. On a hill for pity's sake. What are you now, a size queen? A hill or a mountain, who cares? England's flat. It did its best by you. Why look for something better when what you've got's so beautiful? Take your mountains where you find them."

~~~~~~~~~

Before leaving Scotland, before starting the journey which has become this book, I had a dream. The dream had such resonance that I wrote it down. Some dreams are prophecies. This was one such dream, though I did not know it to be such until it revealed itself in the journey that was still to come. I tell it here, so that its resonance is in place.
~~~~~~~~~

An audience had gathered in a large tent erected on the lawns of a country house. We sat on banks of wooden seating, in front of a cinema screen. This film premiere, of a documentary called *The Spiritual Life*, was the grand finale of this summer festival, but the screen stayed blank. The reels were in place, the projectionist was ready, but the speaker system had failed.

We had the film, but no soundtrack. To the left of the screen was a stepladder. I was asked to mount it and speak the narration.

The film began. An African warrior was standing on one leg, utterly still. His skin was glossy, his body was sleek, naked but for twines of leather and coloured beads. Mountains, dark grey and craggy, ranged around him. Beside him was an expanse of lake, with no breath of wind to stir it. It afforded a clear reflection of both mountains and blue sky.

I had worried that I would not know what to say, but was OK with this opening. I told how this lake without a ripple was Nirvana, the sublime abode of the soul at peace, and that the African was a spiritual warrior.

As the film progressed I found enough to say. Then I sensed we were approaching the grand climax. An aerial shot swept across desert, approaching a range of mountains. I searched the landscape for clues, perhaps an oasis of palm trees or a minaret, something to show me this was the desert of the Holy Land. Perhaps we were flying above Israel and Egypt toward the heights of Mount Sinai.

But I recognized nothing. On the top of my ladder, I perched in awkward silence.

Then my silence became meaningless. My words were not needed. I no longer tried to lead the audience, for I had joined them in a sense of wonder.

The camera looked down on one peak. It was singularly high, rising out of the desert floor, and its top had been sheared at an angle. This plateau of a sheared top had a companion slanted beside it, joined on its right-hand side. The angle of the slope allowed the buildings of this mountaintop to reach above each other, each obtaining a far and expansive view of the earth below.

In form this city was something like the palaces that used to range across the mountainsides of Tibet. However Tibet is old and this was new. These buildings formed a city of a beauty like none I had known. The square form of each building was appealing, but the beauty stemmed from the stone of their composition. This must have been marble, for no other stone has so pure and white a luminescence. The city was large and solid, but this whiteness set it shimmering with an ethereal quality.

The film was over. This mountaintop city was clearly a place of astounding spiritual power yet I had never seen it before. Its image filled the screen as credits in small white letters scrolled across it.

The name of each location appeared, and finally the name I had not known till now.

The Guadalupe Mountains.

I woke the next day and checked for their existence in an atlas. If they existed at all, I guessed they would be South American. In fact the index directed me to the United States and a range of mountains forty miles long, stretching out of New Mexico to push its head into Texas. These were the Guadalupe Mountains.

I had no thought of going there. But years later James had moved to Santa Fe, and I was heading to see him for the summer.

A neighbour was sunbathing on the lawn of the Sussex hillside outside my front door. The sun had burnished his bald head a glossy red. He opened his eyes as my shadow passed across him.

"You've come for me," he said. Sitting up, he opened wide his arms and grinned. "At last. You've seen sense. You can resist my naked body no longer. You're taking me to bed."

I smiled at his joke, and sat down to chat a while. I was about to fly to America, the country of his birth fifty-five years ago. Far from shy in most areas of life, he was also prone to visionary prophecies. Most of these he kept to himself. Knowing the future had not done him much good, but he volunteered some information now, as a parting gift.

"I will tell you this much. There will be one moment in your journey which will change your whole experience of life. I don't want to describe it. Only to say this. I see your feet turn, and the gold dust of angels fly around your ankles."

Prophecies are curious things. They generally seem ridiculous until they come true.

8
Guadalupe Peak
Texas

In Santa Fe, New Mexico, it was Good Friday. In a few weeks' time James would head for Europe, on his way to visiting me in Birling Gap. For now, he had driven up into mountains on the edge of town to camp the night on eleven acres he was thinking of buying. Bears trek across the land, pausing to ruminate by ancient stones with splendid views. A stream winds through wetlands at the lower level. Pinyon and juniper trees wood the slopes, while the meadow above contains a grove of ponderosa trees. They are high altitude trees. Here at 7,500 feet they flourish, reaching fifty feet and dropping a bed of needles to soften the earth below.

This was where James spread his sleeping bag, beside a log fire dug into the ground. The mountain views faded into darkness, stars filled the sky, and he lay down to sleep.

But no sleep came. Instead a voice, the words as silent as words on paper but clear and insistent, pressed a message into his body.

"Bring Martin here," it said.

"No way," he responded. He knew what the voice was implying. This is your hearth, Martin is to be your partner, bring him here to share your whole life with you. The thought was absurd. This wasn't how he thought of me at all. We were good pals, but beyond anything else I wasn't his type. Our conversation was wonderful, but sexually I was a no-go area. He had turned down my invitation to join me on my mountain journeys in India and Sri Lanka, and had even found Glasgow too far away to visit on earlier trips to Europe. He was clear on the man he wanted. Neither blond, nor slight, nor in my twenties, I didn't fit the bill at all.

"Bring Martin here," the voice persisted.

"No."

The debate continued, this voice of the mountain land set against one of the nation's top environmental lawyers. Come three o'clock in the morning, the mountain land won its first concession.

"Well maybe," James allowed.

High in the ponderosa above his head a great-horned howl hooted in victory. James was allowed to fall asleep. When he woke, he found the skull of a mountain lion on the ground near his head.

His current home in Santa Fe was a box-like house with a window that opened onto mountains. James had bought a book to help introduce me to the area, *National Parks of the Southwest*. I opened it at random, straight to the page that introduced Guadalupe National Park. I can be stubborn, the esoteric life is generally so damn subtle, it's easy to stomp across intuitions and carry along the old way regardless. This time the message was so clear as to be brazen. The mountains were calling. That first weekend we packed the camping gear in the car, and drove south.

From the heights of Santa Fe we dropped toward the desert plains of New Mexico. They were like an ocean bed without its sea. Lightning jagged down from the sky to pinpoint the road ahead.

The sun dropped below the land and bats skimmed the roadside, their silhouettes shivering within their speed as they snuffled insects caught against their wings. They poured like smoke out of the Carlsbad Caverns, hundreds of thousands of the creatures streaming from their daytime roost on a ceiling of the western hemisphere's largest sequence of caves. These Caverns are sited within the northern tip of the Guadalupe Mountains. The bats were flagging us down.

A shallow sea used to cover this land that is now shared by the states of New Mexico and Texas. Plant life and creatures gathered at its rim to form a coral reef. Times changed, hundreds of millions of years passed by, and the reef found itself buried thousands of feet below a desert floor. Then we move to comparatively recent times, ten to twelve millions years ago, when the Earth's plates shifted and the reef cracked. The pressure pushed it more than a mile high. Men and women evolved to the level where they could give phenomena a name. The reef that reared to a mile in height was called the Guadalupe Mountains.

We crossed into Texas and pitched camp in Guadalupe National Park. A stag and a skunk sauntered past as we gazed into a black and busy sky. Brief tails of white trailed shooting stars as they arched themselves out of existence.

We scanned the map to see where to climb. The different peaks had many redolent names, often linked to the times when the Apache took shelter in these mountains. Only one was called 'Guadalupe', the name given to me in my dream. This was 'Guadalupe Peak'. The track toward it led from the parking lot and wound round the first broad buttress of a hill to climb out of sight.

Loading ourselves with water, we set out.

James stared intently through his round-rimmed spectacles, like one of his favourite owls, seeking the darting outline of each bird. Birds are one of his passions. Being out in the natural world makes a kid of him again. He skips across undergrowth in pursuit of a beetle, or sits timelessly in front of a flower studying the complement of insect and blossom.

The hands below the cuffs of his shirt, and the face beneath the shadow of his broad-brimmed hat, were both pale. The rest of him remained covered, for his skin flamed red at the touch of the sun. His eyes reflected the light of the landscape, switching from grey to blue to match any blue in the sky.

We walked the first few feet of the mountain trail and our path was crossed by a brown slither of snake.

"A garter snake," James told me.

It served as our starting tape. The ascent had begun.

Fire had swept through the area the previous year to roast some of the cacti where they grew. It reduced some trees to charcoal spindles of themselves, but the fire clung to the desert floor. Some metres higher and the mountain was living again. The sunset red of the bark of the Texan Madrone tree peeled back to reveal golden flesh beneath. Its smooth branches hoisted bundles of dark green leaves in the air, like pom-poms on the naked arms of cheer-leaders.

"Bonsai," James declared, rendering Japanese and possibly Zen the miniature bushes that seeped roots down through hairline cracks in mottled boulders beside the path. Such vegetation was the root of the Bonsai tradition in Japan, he explained. Folk found these miniature growths on top of Japanese mountaintops and carried them home. Their leaves were dark green and shaped like the fingernails of baby dolls, the bushes never more than inches high but sprawling as though each yearned to be a rainforest.

On a fallen tree to the other side a small bird danced and bobbed. It was a canyon wren and I was pleased to meet it, for James had already taught me its song. Clear notes whistled down from perches tucked against the mountainside. They descended a scale to breathe their last in a note that faded into loss.

A bridge of short stout timbers spanned a narrow gorge, and the path wound through high-altitude woodland of Douglas Firs. The summit of 8,749 feet was not far away. The trees sensed the altitude so did not struggle to any great height of their own. Their branches were thick enough to give shade, but sparse enough to let sunlight squeeze through the needles. Chips of white marble were embedded in the path. They caught the sunlight to form a glittering way.

Guadalupe Peak forms the head of its range of mountains, a head that curves round from the red bulk of its body. The path was well-defined and runs at a gentle slope, so it was always a surprise to be able to look down and discover how much height we had gained. The path turned one of its bends and introduced new terrain. The shade of the trees was left behind. We were out in the sunlight once again, and stepping onto a new flank of the mountain that would hold our first view out across to the south.

I stepped backwards to joke with James. We were near the summit. Just a little further and I would have chased my dream to extinction, that dream from Scotland that had pulled me up a Texan mountainside. I laughed and told James to be careful, that I had probably been given this dream so that I could drag him up to this improbable location. He should prepare himself for a revelation.

It was safe to walk backwards because the edge of the path that bordered the drop down the mountain was fringed with bushes. The bushes ended and I turned around.

We had climbed high. Higher than I thought. The view below us included the peak of a mountain. This peak had been sliced away so that it faced us with the steep angle of its slope.

The film that I viewed in my dream had climaxed with the vision of a mountaintop so awesome, so pure, so astonishingly beautiful that my narration was silenced in wonder.

This mountain below me was that exact mountain of my dream. I was viewing it from the very height and angle as were shown in my dream film. There can be nothing more distinctive than the jagged sloping ring of this mountaintop, with a curious buttress like a wing to its right that in my dream housed a secondary city of white. I recognized the mountain at once.

And I was recognized in return.

The vision of the gleaming city of white was a memory from my dream. Instead of the sight of the city I now felt its walls reach around to hold me within themselves. The effect was physical in that my body was overwhelmed by the experience, by the embrace. It was as physical and real and unfathomable as love, a love that rushes in to wrap around your heart and makes you gasp the very best out of yourself.

Waves formed of the substance of love poured from the mountain to meet me.

James reached forward to hold me upright, to stop me from collapsing, then released me slowly. I stepped forward from the path and sat down.

I closed my eyes and opened them. The face of the mountain wobbled at the far side of my tears, cleared itself to stand in its framework of blue sky, then folded itself from sight once more as I was wrapped in a fresh gust of weeping.

My little life, with its hopes and fears and ambitions, wept from me.

A swift passed below my head, the arrow of its body shooting a sound through the air. The bird was gone before the air had time to heal. I watched its flight, an instant swoop down the mountainside then a glide back up to vanish beyond the rim of my mountain face. This mountain face that was now as intimate and real as any face I had known.

This mountain face was so close, a mere second for a swift in flight. If I ran a few steps from where I was standing, I could be there.

Death was as close as that. The time before my birth was as close as that too. This mountain top is the place that I came from, and this is the place I shall return to when I die. I had been brought back to sit in direct contact with the power behind my existence.

James sat some way behind me. He took a photo of me but I have none of him in that moment, so sometimes picture him in his black Zen robes, sitting as solid as a mountain boulder, or maybe as rooted as one of those ancient trees up here that grow to the height of a child and spread whorled boughs to give a shade you can slide beneath.

James spoke of his own experience later. It was an experience of the eternal that he had never known before, of the eternal as something immeasurably deep. While I was being whirled out of all that I knew of my life, he was discovering a reason for his own. This new sense of his incarnation, a reason for his being born, was love. It was love for me, a love beyond emotion, a love that was lodged in his new sense of how deep the eternal is. His new purpose in life was to lead me into a similar field of love, for the joy it could bring me.

I broke away after some time for us to complete the ascent of Guadalupe Peak. The communion with the force of the mountaintop below stayed with me as I moved.

The path forked for this final short climb. A cohort of dragonflies hovered in front of us, flashing their beacons of blue. When they had attracted our attention we proceeded. They wound each turn ahead of us, flying at our walking pace, never hurrying us, never falling behind, leading us higher till we had no more climbing to do.

Flecks of red flew between the dragonfly blue on the summit. I admired these touches of colour as I looked around. To the north of the mountain rose the tree-clad mountains of the Guadalupe range. Salt flats spread across the western view. To the south the light brown stretch of the Chihuahan Desert swept across Texas toward the Mexican border. The south east was studded by the neat cones of small green hills.

There below us, of course, was my mountaintop. A brief rush of air came behind me as I looked down, a zip of energy, and a dragonfly bounced off the crown of my head. And across my chest, in a pattern that moved and thickened, some red flecks from the air had settled to pad through the salt of my sweat.

They were ladybirds. Almost everything was ladybirds. They formed a heaving cover to leaves and twigs and branches and stones. This was an emergence of them. The call had gone out over the Lord knows how many states and they had swarmed in to this highest point of Texas. Texan insects congregate in style. Stay still and we could hear them, racing over each other's brittle bodies to find a slot and drop into the orgy. The click click click of a million feet rattled beneath the reddened twigs of a bush and we looked in on a wooden box. These creatures rode across the pine of its casing, a living crust an inch high as they humped and mounted each other. The brown casings of last year's bodies were heaped on the ground, within the bush's shade.

"They're beautiful," James said, bowing down to admire the red clusters on my knees. "Like decorations by Fabergé."

I brushed the ladybirds from my legs, and climbed down a few steps to picnic on a sandwich beneath a tree on the far side of the mountain. A beetle with a luminous blue back appeared and performed a dance in the dust at our feet, its feet spinning it round in crazy circles while its wings shivered in the air.

I sensed it was dying and focused attention on it. The dance subsided, the beetle grew still, and it let itself die with some peace. The body deserved rest. I took a few stones and leaned them against each other around the insect, then set another on top to roof the miniature tomb.

We stood and began our walk down.

I settled myself on a white boulder, sitting once again in the place my dream had brought me .

"There's no need to hurry," James advised from behind.

I stood to go, and reached the path. Turning to face my mountain in goodbye a cool wind rushed up through the stillness of air. I held out my arms and laughed into the wind before crying again and going back to my boulder.

"Is there anything else I should do?" I asked aloud.

James's voice answered me after a while.

"Ask the spirits and guardians of the place for any understanding they can give."

The suggestion felt right, and I made the silent request. Love surged toward me with greater strength. It was as though many beings were glad to be recognized as individuals. They were pulsing their individual beams of response.

I have been told a shaman's story of beings who came to Earth, some from nearby and some from far away. They landed on a mountain top and were so astonished by the beauty of the planet that they could do nothing but stay and worship it. The story could be true of these beings of Guadalupe. They seemed to thrill to the beauty of existence.

The shearing of this peak below me formed a plain. This flat mountain top was grey with jagged edges as the rim of its world, and coated with the soft green of Douglas Firs. I looked down and could see it was accessible. I could manage the walk. I could return to this plain that was my home.

Only one thread of logic stopped me going, a thin thread that I could trail through my fingers to guide me back down the mountainside and away. If I was here before my birth, the logic kept repeating, then there must be a reason for my having been sent away. I was out in some mission in life, not some feeble mission of my own invention but one that was planted in me. I had been brought back here to be reminded of this fact, to tune in once more to the degree of love that was behind me. With such assurance of this love, I was to step back into my life once again.

The steps back down the mountain involved an acceptance of being born again. Only this time the birth was not as a baby but as an adult.

I thought I was strong enough, and turned the corner where the path drops between the trees, but my grief at leaving was too strong. I collapsed against a rock, gasped at the air, and let my cries come out as howls.

"Sing," James suggested. "Could you sing it out?"

Leaning on a tree below the path I opened my mouth. Great resonant sounds swelled out, deep notes at first then higher till the song reached a pitch from which it came quavering down through my jaw. They were strange sounds I had never encompassed before, a song that left me clear.

I was able to go back to the corner and bid a more controlled farewell. This was one of those gentle mistakes that destiny allows. James had an esoteric passion drawn from the Japanese part of his being of which I had never heard. The Japanese call the art suiseki, and its practitioners are hallowed as special members of society. The sport involves assembling rocks in a garden, each of which has within its essence all the qualities of a whole mountain range. James now took time to seek such a piece.

"Look," he sang out as I came back down the path.

He was an Atlas on the path of Zen, straining the muscles of his arms to lift his latest miniature mountain range into the air.

"I think we can get it down, can't we?"

The rock filled the backpack. It lent its weight to gravity and helped us back down to earth.

We took a short drive through the Chihuahan Desert to look up from the roadside at the giant pillar of red rock that supports my mountaintop. It has the name El Capitan and rises sheer. Its highest point is 8,085 feet. Red earth sweeps up to form its apron, held in place by a natural fortified wall of red rock, then the paler monolith soars beyond. It is formidable, one of the mightiest rocks I have seen. Navajo Indians call monoliths like these 'sky-supporters', warriors frozen in stone who will come to the protection of those who approach them in the right way.

The roadside view was impressive, but the tower of rock does not transmit the same power as I felt when facing the other side. It is the slanting face of El Capitan that transmits the love to me, the sloping top of the monolith. El Capitan is a vast column that holds up this plain of existence. In such a way it truly is a 'sky-supporter', for the only term I have to describe this mountaintop is heaven. Heaven is in the sky, and this mountaintop is heaven on earth.

A curious cloud formation marked the otherwise clear blue sky as I sat at our campsite and looked up. Two wisps, one curled into a semi-circle and the other floating nearby as a small blob, just needed a fractional adjustment to form a question mark.

I waited by our tent till night then wandered off in the dark, walking down the road till I could see the silhouette of my mountaintop. I had some questions for it.

"Why can't I stay here?" I asked. "What's the point of living any more?"

The answer that came back was a cliché, and a sentimental one at that.

"All you need is love," the mountain said.

The words were pressed silently in my heart. I could hear the mountain voices well now, just as the mountain could read my thoughts. Our dialogue was truly open.

Now we were in dialogue, I wished for something better. I heard "All you need is love" as a kid from the Beatles. I wanted something more unique, more explicit.

"Do you remember snippets about love from recent conversations?" the query came back. "Things that James has said?"

“But they were nothing. Just two people struggling with words. You’ve shown me what love is now. It’s something far beyond that. Can’t I stay?”

"Go back," the mountain insisted. "OK, so that talk of love is confused when you think of it now, but it was beautifully lucid at times. Go back. Carry on the conversation. Look at love again and see what you can discover on that human level. Believe us, it’s worth a try."

“OK. I’ll go back to my life, but there has to be a deal. You’ve brought me back. You must stay with me now, even when I walk away. You must make sure I never forget you again.”

"It’s a deal," the mountain replied.

Up in the night sky I saw a single shooting star. It performed a somersault, its trail forming a brief white loop, before it expired.

In the morning we packed away the tent then walked over the low ridge of a nearby hill. Mistletoe garlanded the branches of a tree which dropped shade onto the desert floor. I sat in this shade and looked out. I had come to view my mountaintop for one more time, and sought some final understanding to take with me.

The understanding came. It breezed in with the sight of a large bird of prey that was gliding from the desert to curve its flight around El Capitan.

"Here comes an image," the silent voices from the mountain say. "One that can settle in your human mind. One you can transmit so that others can understand. Are you ready?"

I waited. The message came.

"Do you think that bird gives a thought to its flight? Of course not. It adjusts its wings and rides on currents of air it cannot see. Be like that bird. Feel these waves of love that come from our mountain, and let them carry you through your life.”

McKittrick Canyon cuts into the Guadalupe Mountains. Its river sets the desert sprouting green. We walked into it on our way back north into New Mexico. I caught a movement between the slender grey trunks of trees, a lean body sprung on sinewy legs. It moved silently and swiftly. It was a mountain lion. One glimpse, then it was gone.

~~~~~~~~~~

Does the world need this story?

I take guidance from the fact that within my dream the soundtrack had failed. I was asked to narrate the wonders of a film to the audience who were waiting for it. It is a story that needs to be told.

So one hope I have for the astonishing story of Guadalupe Peak and sacred mountains is that readers begin to see mountains as beings. We get to move while they stay still, but they are great teachers. They transmit a power that can steer us through our lives.

The mountain journey of this book would continue. It would reveal how Guadalupe is vital for the regeneration of the whole planet, unleashing a latent power in North America that will help that nation lead the way.

Such things, of course, are hard to believe. They seem to belong to a time of fairytales and dragons. And indeed one of the closest things to a dragon the area has to offer was waiting to impart secrets on my very next mountain outing.
~~~~~~~~~~

9
Chaco Canyon
New Mexico

Experts pretend to have fathomed the mysteries of Chaco Canyon. They brush away the dust of more than a thousand years, examine these great ruins of an Indian civilization, and judge that this was the principal area for trade among the Indian settlements of the region. The circular chambers dug deep into the ground were for storage of grain. The tracery of paths that run like spokes across the desert plains all around, homing in on this central point, were made by the passage of Indian traders and their goods.

As a home for five thousand people, there is a lot for archaeologists to discover about the social and commercial organization of life in the canyon. The alternative facts of the area's spiritual dimension have been harder to grasp.

In the 1970s some advance was made with a woman's discovery while climbing the top of Fajada Butte, a mighty monolith of red stone that rises sheer and high from the canyon's floor. Noticing how a beam of sun struck a distinctive portion of the rock, her awareness broadened. Soon she was able to see how the whole summit of the Butte was as an ancient astronomical clock tuned to the solstices.

James and I entered by the dust track which is the road in from the north, and would leave by the dust track which is the road in from the south. We were no experts, not even amateurs. We didn't know what to look for.

Perhaps that's why we found out something new.

There is a wall to one of the buildings of Chaco Canyon, Pueblo Bonito, that I am told by someone who channels such information is a 'healing wall', a 'wall of love'. It is built without cutting stones, without clamping them together. Long, thin, flat stones were gathered by master masons and assembled so that each stone found its surrounding partners, settled into the perfect fit, and the mass of such harmony grew into the great curved wall of this building.

I was told too of a lady who knew nothing of the properties of this wall but brought a sickness with her on a visit to Chaco Canyon. She was asked to place her hands on the wall and stay in silence for a while. On leaving the Canyon she pronounced herself cured.

As James and I approached the wall we both remarked on a sense of entering a presence, an aura of spiritual dimension. It was as though this wall had an outer etheric wall which we could step inside. Standing in the early sunlight with my hands on its stone, fresh from our tent and the Pueblo's first visitors since dawn, I felt some strong movement and pressure within the right side of my face. Maybe it was working away at obstacles so that I might smile more easily. I could think of no specific healing that I needed, but I was glad of whatever help toward love a loving wall could give me.

These various buildings, each a self-contained village or *pueblo*, once reached three stories high. Each was home for up to a thousand people. Kivas drop their bodies into the earth, round subterranean wombs where people once gathered in worship of their gods. One complex of their ruins, now known as Kin Kletso, lies beside the cliff wall of the North Mesa to catch what it can of shade. Behind this a path of hewn stairs climbs up a narrow fissure in the cliff face. It leads up to the table-land of the North Mesa. It affords an aerial view of the various pueblos shaped like amphitheatres, a semi-circle of buildings each spanning a straight fronting wall.

Heading anti-clockwise, following the arrows that mark this Mesa-top walk, the first such pueblo is Pueblo Arroyo. The official booklet to this Pueblo describes its mystery;

"The orientation of Pueblo Arroyo [*arroyo* being the local Spanish term for a channel that receives the sudden flash-flood streams of the rains] differs from most other great houses because it faces east rather than south, and it is one of few in the canyon set out in the open flood plains away from the cliffs."

This strange positioning, the booklet tells us, remains a mystery.

I looked out, above Pueblo del Arroyo and beyond, through a broad gap in the South Mesa where the canyon stretches to the east. In a direct line at a distance of some miles is a cluster of flat-topped mountains, Hosta Buttes, the central one of which is majestic and high. It seemed very clear to me why Pueblo del Arroyo was sited just where it is, and no mystery at all. It reached out the arms of its rear wall to collect and embrace the power pouring from this gathering of mountains.

I had my intuition. Now I needed an expert in the field to confirm it.

Circling the table-top of this Mesa, past a splendid view down over Pueblo Bonito, the path rises through brush to the Mesa's highest point. Pueblo Alto ('high village'), formerly of 135 rooms, is the complex that crowns this piece of land. The ground is rich in pottery shards and the walls have crumbled to a foot or two in height.

Battered by the heat of the sun I moved for the shelter of the more extant walls in the nearby ruins of New Alto. James darted off on a curiously direct route across the brush to the base of Pueblo Alto's mound. Some minutes later he called to me. I hauled myself over to see what he had found.

A creature sat motionless on a rock. It accepted my approach, and gave me time to admire it. It was about seven inches long plus the balance of a long, fine tail. Its heels rested on the rock and its long yellow toes tapered into the air to keep clear of the earth's burning surface. Its toes were like the delicate hands and fingernails of a Chinese mandarin.

It was a collared lizard. Its collar was like an Elizabethan ruff, its colours the range of brilliance of the sky from the sun's yellow to the clearness of its blue. It had been training itself in grace since primordial times.

Sure of our attention, secure in our admiration, it climbed from its rock and scuttled a short way up the path, its feet clicking against the stones.

Twenty feet ahead of us now it paused and looked back over its shoulder. We were stupid but the lizard had patience. When we cottoned on to what was expected of us and started to follow, it waited till we were close behind it then clicked on once again.

Up the slope we went, into the ruins where we paused to draw breath, then set off on one final guided spurt. The lizard sped up to the top of the outer wall and perched there.

This was our destination. We crouched by the lizard's side, prepared for further moves, but the creature was now motionless. It kept its gaze fixed firmly across the plain.

Pueblo Alto shares the same alignment as Pueblo Arroyo down below, but at this height the reason for it was apparent. Straight ahead of us was the distinctive shape of the Hosta Buttes. Settled in the forcefield, its toes raised as though transmitting magic of its own in reply, the lizard was rapt in front of the distant mountain.

I had found my expert. My intuition was confirmed. Thankful for the lesson, we stepped gently away.

~~~~~~~~~

From Chaco Canyon we headed west for Mount Taylor, supremely sacred to the Navajo Indians. The mountain is a dark mass, its summit a classically formed pointed peak.

It seemed foreboding.

Our plan to climb it evaporated. We parked the car a while, stared upwards, then drove on. I read a passage about Mount Taylor the following night.

Uranium mining was still active on its western slopes. Directed by the Chevron corporation this used to be the site of the most concentrated uranium mining in all of North America. It was now coated in radioactive soil and dust. On its eastern side an open-pit uranium mine had polluted the drinking waters of the Laguna Pueblo, the home of Indians who hold the sacredness of this mountain and its waters as central to their beliefs.

Our instincts had spared us a hike through radioactive dust. Mount Taylor, the mightiest element in a strong landscape, one of the holiest places on the planet, has been poisoned. Drop radioactive waste into our cathedrals, stuff it for safekeeping in their crypts, and the world would be ablaze with horror and fury. Nothing is larger or more magnificent than our mountains, but we hold them in such scant respect we pay no heed to their desecration.

"I told them so," a collared lizard may one day say, when humans are extinct. "They have no excuses. I pointed across the desert right at one of the mountains. 'Look at that!' I said. 'It's the secret of life. It's what keeps us all on course. Tune yourself to its frequency and we'll all be safe.' But would they listen?"
~~~~~~~~~

We headed west, across Arizona and into California. James wanted to take me to an area where the mountains had first spoken to him, written about in his own book *A Field Guide to the Soul.* A voice had boomed down at him from out of the skies.

We were heading for a powerful mountain kingdom.

10
Sierra Nevada
California

The wings of a Stellar's jay flashed blue between the trees to lead us from our tent toward a mountain stream. The stream ran fast in the form of water, and above it ran another stream we could not see but only feel. A stream of air. It cooled itself on fields of snow then skimmed down from the heights, whisking scents from meadows and trees and ancient wood, the essence of all the scenery rushed into a wind that buffed the sides of our faces like a mother's waking caress.

We walked up from our parking place at Mosquito Flats -- so basic and redolent, these American names -- and began a sequence of views whose beauty was unprecedented in my life. Up in these heights panoramas never trouble to repeat themselves, but simply spin fresh landscapes from an eternal source of wonders. You follow the path over one high horizon and into the details of another view that spreads itself wide to astonish. It is like a sequence of set designs for high-romantic opera.

A small animal is unique to the scree at this height. In that curious manner of rodents it can fold its body over the hard edges and angles of rocks, travelling like a shadow, and slide within cracks to shelter from predators. It looks like a mouse, but is the size of one that has swallowed a guinea pig. Its life of moulding its soft body around hard rocks finds expression in the creature's voice, a shrill cry like a bird's.

It is called a pika.

I first saw one crest the waves of granite rocks that had tumbled to the left of the path. Then I traced a cry to find another sitting down to the right, daring to raise its head for a view above the shallow waters of a lake to the mountains beyond.

It was a funny creature. Its whistle of a voice set me doing strange things with my own. As we turned for Chicken Foot Lake and entered the path up toward Morgan's Pass my voice sank to a *basso profondo* and practiced operatic declamations of nonsense in Italian.

"*Sono un uomo come una montagna è una montagna*," I let boom. "I am a man like a mountain is a mountain."

My voice switched into song. Maintaining its unfamiliar bass it rendered Sarastro's song at the end of *The Magic Flute,* 'In den Heiligen Hallen', the song that accompanies Tamino and Tamina on their ritual walk of purification at the opera's close. It became vital to me that this song be sung as I trod into this final high valley.

"That's wonderful," James commented from behind. "Have you ever heard my Queen of the Night?"

It is a song for a stabbing soprano. James held up both hands, the fingers clamped to a point as though he were plucking the high notes from the sky. He paused.

"It's gone," he said. "How odd. I can't remember a note of it."

He tried a while longer.

"No. It's no use. It's logical, I suppose. We're *in den Heiligen Hallen* after all. We're in Sarastro's court. There's no way the Queen of the Night could enter here."

He spread his arms and turned a slow circle to honour the mountains that surrounded us. They are formed of pure granite, their lines sharp and their composure complete.

We neared the entrance to the Pass, a passage into months of wilderness walking for those who dare. Many of the mountains within this range stand without names, the human traffic among them so minimal, the range so vast.

The path curls around to a point where it loses its definition. I turned to face the vast granite pyramid of the mountain that lay in front of me. A special awe is invoked by the sense of a mountain composed of a single piece of stone.

Something in this mountain forced me to absorb its qualities as my own. I stood and felt some transformation take effect. I began to become whole, to become immovable. The process started in my head, blanking out whatever element of my brain might prompt me to movement. This was the end of my ascent for the day. This was my goal. I turned around and sat on a wayside stone for a while, staring up at this mountain in reverence.

I met the same inability to move, the same tendency to tears, the same mute facing of a mountain that had enveloped me on Guadalupe. It was a further communion with a power of love. I did not sense it as coming from the spirits of a mountaintop this time. The transmission seemed to be of the essence of the mountain itself. Wonder was at play here, an almighty reassurance that the power I thought I had left behind at Guadalupe was still with me.

James paused, leaving me space and time till I could stand again.

It was too soon to leave this granite mountain, yet I no longer needed to sit still. I now understood that the love of mountains could stay with me wherever I went. The time was ripe to celebrate this happy realization with a ritual.

I am English. James has Irish ancestry, and his homecomings from school in Queens were always signalled by the steam from his mother's fresh pot of hot tea. The Japanese side of his Zen training had lent a new dimension to his love of tea.

It was tea-time.

I looked for a spot on the mountainside to sit and pour from our thermos flask of Fortnum and Mason's First Flush Darjeeling, accompanied by a slice of Betty's Finest Fruit Cake brought from a teashop in York.

"Step this way," I called up to James.

Sensing something special, he took off his hat to let his short black hair spring up and greet the sun for a while. He stepped gracefully, setting his feet on the flat stones that had been placed by nature to pave a gradual descent.

"Now look here.... " I instructed. "Now look there."

He turned obediently to admire the fresh view of a mountain that was granted on every step, and greeted each one with a gentle smile.

"Look at this."

A pattern of small stones, each with its separate pattern of colours, had been laid down to ornament a boulder.

"Now please sit here."

Our picnic site was a broad flat stone that was filled with the warmth of the day. Just ahead of us and to the left was a tangle of wood, stripped of its bark by the force of some mountain stream. It stood yellow, its separate branches linked into a sculpture of great beauty. A flow of mountain water had set out the whole of this picnic site for us.

"It's a Japanese rock garden. Isn't it all perfect?" I said, pleased to have matched the path and the garden with this aspirant Zen monk who was so perfectly trained to tread and appreciate it.

We sipped our tea, nibbled our cake, and absorbed the sweep of a view that was the valley below.

My steps back down the mountain path were not steps back into an old way of life. I might have thought that in Guadalupe, but now it had been proved that the mountain's power of love was not only behind me but also some way ahead.

My way of walking changed. I had tried walking meditations in the past, seeing if I could hypnotize myself by gazing at the steady trudge of my own feet. The practice bored me. Now each step was as though I was treading into the fullness of the world around me. Shift through several gears inside my head, gears that were located somewhere near the temples -- first gear, second gear, third gear -- and I was walking 'mindfully', each step an entry into the same space I had inhabited with the mountain.

I slipped out of this state at times to take a simple, effortless stroll, then slipped into it again, following the river and its broad steps of lakes, the valley shaded with trees and grasses and flowers like a carpet of everything that was comfortable and good.

We found three children sitting by the side of the path, the backpacks beside them almost bigger than their bodies. The two boys were aged about eleven. One, the most tired of all, was dark and sturdy. A baseball cap was squeezed around the crewcut of his head and sweat rimmed his face. He was from Hawaii, and gasping at the altitude.

The other boy was slight, with bright blue eyes and a thick mop of golden hair above a translucent face. He was the leader. The other child was his sister, slighter still with hair about her shoulders and eyes that blinked slowly with tiredness. They feared they could not now reach Chicken Foot Lake where they wished to camp, and that their sense of being lost would soon overwhelm them in the darkness of night.

They smiled at our assurance that they were almost there, gripped on to the security of our map, hid themselves beneath their packs, and walked on up the path.

The children were innocence at its most trusting and brave.

"They were the chorus," James said. "The chorus of three children from *The Magic Flute*. The opera is complete."

I picked up a small stone by the side of the path, wanting to feel its warmth. It was cold. I clasped it tight within my hands, and breathed warm air across it, seeing if I could give it some heat of my own.

Then it was time to put the stone back down.

I looked as I walked to see if there was a perfect place. To the left of the path, for some unknown reason, was a ring of small stones such as mine. With delight I placed my stone at its centre.

It was a tiny incident, my relationship with this small stone, but it had about it a surprising perfection.

I paused at several points on the way down to Mosquito Flats, stilled by the mountains once again and brought to the point of tears for love and remembrance. The sun was now setting to pour in a special magic of light, burnishing the grey hides of the mountains and discovering veins streaked into their granite sides.

I slipped through those gears again to enter that state of mindfulness as I walk to the close of the path. Just before the car park I turned to face a peak of mountain now turned golden above the trees.

I studied the scene for a moment, then closed my eyes.

A russet pyramid of mountain, with the dark green of fir trees around its base, ceased being still and began to swirl as atoms. The colours became disconnected, like tiny brush strokes of a pointillist painting, and the mountain became fluid. I stood within its stream as the mountain poured into me.

Stand or kneel, open my eyes or close them again, so long as I stayed the process continued. The mountain poured into me. The mountain and I merged.

My wish on Arunachala had come true. I had become like a mountain. The love that had come from outside of me was inside of me now.

I now know something of how Hindus worship stones, of how Ramana Maharshi hugged a stone to his body and knew life as complete. When I hear it said that someone has a heart of stone I shall seek to love them, for stone can run as energy and love.

~~~~~~~~~

One trick I've learned about writing books: You don't put the climax at the very end. Something big may happen there, but if so it's like an aftershock. If your book's going to quake, it should be in the penultimate chapter or so. The reader then has time to ride the experience toward the close.

I suspect Dr. W.Y.Evans-Wentz was not interested in such tricks of the trade. He wandered the Orient in the early twentieth century, and his translation was the first to bring *The Tibetan Book of the Dead* to Western readers. Read the books of conversations with Ramana Maharshi and you will find him in those pages too, stopping by the guru's ashram on his visit to Arunachala. When he climbed Adam's Peak his timing was better than mine and he saw the dawn.

He was a wealthy man who chose to live alone in a boarding house in San Diego. Part of his family inheritance was a ranch in Baja California, the broad swathe of land that straddles the border between Mexico and the USA. A dominant feature on this ranch was Mount Tecate, which Evans-Wentz preferred to call by its Native American name of Cuchama. He told the story in his book, *Cuchama and Sacred Mountains*.

I knew nothing of Cuchama, and next to nothing about Evans-Wentz, when I walked into City Lights Bookstore in San Francisco. It was a good raid. I had several unknown books in my hand as I wandered up the stairs to the till, but something made me turn around and burrow through the shelves again. An extra piece of magic had to be hidden somewhere in that cellar of fascinating books.
~~~~~~~~~

My hand homed straight in and slid *Cuchama and Sacred Mountains* off the shelf. Evans-Wentz was dead, but even so I was delighted at finding such a companion on my quest. His journey parallelled mine, and Cuchama was an especially thrilling discovery. I was due to drop James off at a Zen mountain retreat, which would leave me with a week to kill in Los Angeles. Cuchama suddenly offered itself as a sacred mountain to complete my journey.

Evans-Wentz came to view Cuchama as the equal to all the sacred mountains he had visited around the world. In tandem with that realization was another which has special impact considering he was one of the foremost Oriental scholars of his day. He had been absorbed by the wisdom contained in the writings of the greatest Indian and Chinese sages. Now he saw that these enlightened Oriental perspectives were more like stepping stones toward the degree of cosmic understanding achieved by Native American Indians. He contended that these Native Americans drew on the strata of spiritual power that covered their country. This same strata of spirituality was there for others to draw on too, if only they could become aware of it.

This was fascinating enough. An addendum at the back of the book then broke the bounds of fascination. For me it has become the most intriguing snippet in world literature. My experience on Guadalupe Peak had been phenomenal. This passage in the book was clearly smaller, but it was small like the match is small that you light and bring to a fuse. The combination of my dream, of the mountaintop, and of this information, has the capacity to reformulate the planet.

Cuchama and Sacred Mountains was edited by Frank Waters, a writer who dedicated his life to the mountains and native culture of the South West. The addendum was his. It dealt with a booklet that Evans-Wentz had sent him to back his belief in a pan-American Indian Renaissance.

The booklet was called *The Coming of the Great White Chief*. In Frank Water's words: "It described a secret, ancient city in the mountains of southern Mexico inhabited by white-skinned Chigarau Indians ruled by a Great White Chief, who prophesied the amalgamation of all Indians under his teachings. The amalgamation purportedly had begun at the First Inter-American Indian Conference in Patzcuaro where the Great White Chief had informed the delegates that the time had come to build a magnificent Indian capitol. Five quarries in Central America had been selected to provide white marble for the temple. Soon the transportation of the marble and the migration of tribes toward the north would begin. The tribes would cross the Rio Grande River and journey west toward a range of mountains on which only the morning sun would shine. There they would build the Great White City with its white marble temple."

Frank Waters had attended that conference, and his initial reaction was to find the contents of the booklet wholly spurious. However he debated the issue and was led to view the establishment of this mountain city not as something physical, but as something spiritual. It would mark what he saw as the 'Sixth Age of Consciousness' as prophesied in writings from the Mayan civilization.

The conclusion reached by Evans-Wentz, Waters and their correspondents, was that Indian civilization had been decimated to a point from which it could not regenerate fast enough to hold back the ravages of the planet. It would need people with deep experience of old Indian civilization to reincarnate in white skins. They must then access the strata of wisdom that covers North America, a strata transmitted by the country's mountains.

I have been primed to discount such writing as hokum, but as I read the prophecy of a white mountain city my heart beat fast. It was the shock of recognition. I remembered Guadalupe, and the dream that had originally taken me there. It was a dream of a great white city, built on a mountain top that was sheathed at an angle and set to face East.

I am unsure about the distinction between spiritual and physical, but the great white city exists. I saw it in my dream. I was drawn across the world to experience its very real presence and absorb its impact in my body. I sat and looked down on the site of the city, on a mountaintop beyond the Rio Grande. I watched it receive the morning sun.

I telephoned Frank Waters some months before his death. We spoke of Cuchama and he remembered the mountain fondly, but he had forgotten details of the booklet. I thanked him for the inspirational example of his writings and his life. Toward the close of his addendum he wrote of 'the still grievous imbalance between Indians and Whites throughout the Americas. Their conflict is rooted in their inherently different views of nature and man. It has resulted in the tragic dominance of materialistic Western civilization over naturalistic Indian society, to the detriment of both.'

For myself, the establishment of a spiritual city in the Guadalupe mountains is a fact. It can help steer us toward a balanced evolution of our planet. If we stay blinkered to the power of the natural world we will be excluded. The planet will continue without us. The promise of Guadalupe is that it is not too late. We can change the values by which we steer our lives, and America can lead the way. The choice is ours.

I headed down the Pacific Coast to find out what Cuchama might have to teach us.

11
Cuchama
Baja California

A popular comment when people talk about their favourite mountains is that these mountains were once higher than the Himalayas. The Alps were once higher than the Himalayas. So were the Scottish Highlands. These are mountains worn down by the ages so that they are now much closer to their essence. By comparison the Himalayas are upstarts.

Cuchama is another example of these ancient mountains, once many times its current height of 3,887 feet. The Indian name Cuchama translates as 'exalted high place'. The tradition was for an elder to lead young Indian males up to the summit and leave them there to sit, without clothing, for one or two nights. This was their initiation into manhood. During the course of the night they would discover the identity of their power animal that would guide them through life, and wake from their dreams with the knowledge of their vocation. With the dawn that followed this revelation they would return down the mountain and assume their new role within their community.

Though shorter than of old, the mountain is still obvious enough. Or so you would think.

I still wonder how I missed it first time round.

The Mexican town of Tecate was busy running around itself in the aftermath of a recent general election. The town streets were lined with square white buildings, their cinder blocks just a little out of joint and awaiting rendering. They served as the shops, the hotels and banks. Beyond this commercial district were the same white buildings, only decreasing in size. At first they were houses, and then they were hovels. I drove between them in a puzzled quest for my latest sacred mountain.

A fair selection of hills surrounded the town, but each looked as scrubby as the other. I could run up and down every one of them in the course of an afternoon. Only one of the mountains in view was clearly mighty, one of those mothering peaks with a tidy head and a long ridge like arms spread wide. The only problem was that this was over on the Californian side of the border, back in the United States.

I took out the book that had led me here, *Cuchama and Sacred Mountains* by W.Y. Evans-Wentz, to see if it offered any clues.

It did.

There was a photograph taken from the north. A description stated that the bulk of the mountain and its peak were on United States' territory while only the southern slope reached into Mexico. The final clue, fairly conclusive, was a map. It marked the dirt road that led to the mountain, just inside the US border.

I drove back to the border crossing.

"Why the hurry?" the US immigration official asked. He pulled my passport out of my hand and into the safety of his booth.

"I've got to climb a mountain," I told him. "I thought it was in Mexico but it's not. It's right behind you. I've only been out of the country ten minutes."

He wouldn't return my passport. I pulled in with my car and a new official came over.

"Where are you going?"

"Cuchama," I said. This old Indian name did not seem to mean much so I tried the new one on him, the geographer's name for the mountain. "Mount Tecate. Do you know it? It's over there, look. That is it, isn't it? And here it is too, in this book."

I opened my book on its map and began to explain my whole story.

"Put it away."

He waved the book aside. I opened the page that showed the photo.

"Put it away. I'm not interested. This is an inspection. Stop talking. It's me who asks the questions."

A black labrador sniffed the car for anything illicit. Finding nothing, it thrust its snout into a nearby soldier's knapsack then snorted round his trouser cuffs. The dog handler pulled the chain to drag the dog away. The search of my car found nothing more intriguing than a few pinyon logs for a possible camp fire. My stories checked out. My passport was returned.

"Thank you, sir," the official said. "Have a nice day."

The car spat dust along the track that runs along the US side of the border, a border formed from old fencing of corrugated iron sheets. The Mexican town of Tecate was squeezed tight against the other side, but on this side the countryside was empty. The only regular users of this road were the border patrols.

And wildlife. A creature ran splay-footed in front of the car. Its chest was puffed out and its wings tucked in as it stormed along. Then with a bound, and a few messy flaps, it gave up the race and leapt from the earth to take roost on a branch of a leafless tree.

It was a roadrunner. Its run was great fun to watch, pure Charlie Chaplin. I wanted more. I wanted to see it jump down and race down the road once again.

It blinked, slow blinks of its big round eyes, and flicked its head between its possible angles of escape, but it had no way out. I stood at the base of its tree.

Something distracted my attention. I turned to look up into the sky behind me. A golden eagle was soaring down from the heights of Cuchama. I followed its flight till it dropped over the border and into the Mexican town, then turned back to my roadrunner.

There's a confederacy amongst birds.

The tree was bare. The eagle had acted as a decoy. The roadrunner was gone.

It is a curiosity about this mountain that nobody I spoke to in the neighbourhood knew its name - neither as Cuchama nor Mount Tecate. I asked the immigration officials, the girls in the grocers, the men hauling scrap from a wasteground at the foot of the mountain itself. It was a relief to park the car in a small grove, opposite a field filled with the border patrols' German Shepherd dogs. My parking space was labelled with letters painted onto a whitewashed boulder. *Pilgrims' Grove, Mount Cuchama.* The dogs flung themselves against the mesh fencing as I started on my climb.

To get to the top of a mountain you have to go up. It is the equivalent of walking into the sun to keep a sense of direction, hard going but sure. Finding no one path to follow but countless little ones, lines of bare earth where the tangle of bushes and trees failed to join, I assured myself I was on course so long as I was going uphill. Up I went, ever upwards, working my way around outcrops of rock and sometimes pausing in their shade before clambering on again. I was walking alone and felt the lack of James. I had grown used to his naming the vegetation for me and making sense of the landscape. Instead he was settled into the rigours of a Zen retreat on the flank of a distant mountain.

My hand reached up to pull me higher. My fingers pressed small stones into dust. I was holding on to a different surface. Up went my head, up went my feet, and I was standing on a road.

It was a dirt road, single track, built to service the meteorological station on the summit. One of the curiosities of the region is that though lightning is common it has never been known to strike Cuchama, and so meteorologists set out to study the phenomenon. This road is part of the same desecration of the mountain as the squat cement buildings of the weather station on the summit.

As with many such dubious advances of mankind, I enjoyed its benefits. My mountain pilgrimage became a patient walk along gentle slopes as the road wound back and forth above itself. Most of the drama of the natural world was swept away when the road was built. A couple of tiny lizards skittered across the path, and I met one most curious black spider. It shunted itself from side to side, uncertain whether any one way was better than any other. It had what looked like a white feather strapped across the top of it, one tuft covering its back and the other its head. James told me later it was a wolf spider. Dressed like that, it was a wolf spider in sheep's clothing.

The view of the summit from below, of a summit that rises into one tidy peak, changed as I drew near. That peak, crowned by the abandoned weather station with wires hammered into a large crucifix on its roof, is indeed the highest point but is part of a ridge all of which could be said to be the top. I left the road to find my own path, and chose an undeveloped part on which to sit.

The climb was not strenuous, but it had brought me to a point that lay up above a mountainous world. California looking northwards was range after range of bald brown hills, many handsome in form but all some way below. It was a land without people. To the south as well the high land of Mexico was there to look down on, highways skirting mountainsides to bring goods through this town of Tecate that huddled against the United States border.

Scrubby bushes grew across the summit. Inside a ring of their shelter, and with the naked vision quests of Indian youths in my mind, I took off my clothes and sat to rest in the heat. A smooth and slanted rock made it easy for me to cross my legs and sit with my back straight, and my face turned toward the sun. The wind breathed through the heat to greet me.

I was tired. My head began to nod. Remembering that those Indian youths sought wisdom in their dreams, I let the waves of slumber come. The rock was smooth enough to lay back on. My hat spread shade across my face. I was asleep.

My mountain journey was beginning to take some toll on my senses. I began to suspect, and also to fear, that I was to be a prophet of a new world order. Zoroaster, Mohammed, Moses, even Joseph Smith of the Mormons took some sense of mission up into the mountains and came down to found new religions. They were normal men, surprised out of their skin by the power of revelation. So why not me too?

I do not know how long, or where, sleep took me. It was a journey far beyond the black realm of the inside of my hat. I woke, pulled the hat from my face, and sat up to face the sun. I was wrapped in a delicious sense of calm. I was not to be quaked open and consequently start a new religion, as I had feared. I was not to be shattered. The sun was dropping but still lent me its warmth. The folds of the hills below were brushed with mist and all of them were gentle. A great peace existed in simply sitting here, and knowing it a beautiful place to be.

The restlessness that had stirred me into my pilgrimage through sacred mountains had passed. My journey felt complete. Cuchama offered me a moment of arrival. I recognized this moment. Along with the recognition came the ability to honour it in some way.

I used to think that sacred ritual belonged to priests and shamans. I could now see that I was wrong. A ritual arose from within me as a response to the sacredness of the space and the moment. A ceremony opened itself out of a deep sense of thankfulness. I was thankful for my journey, and thankful for its span across the Earth. I was thankful for the peace of the present moment.

I sat first to send some memories into the sun and the wind, recalling with thanks the mountains of my journey. The vision of Ararat streamed down from the skies, and folded around the images of each of the other mountains along my way. Around Croagh Patrick. Around Arunachala. Around Adam's Peak. Around Guadalupe. Places and moments returned as memories to pulse me their warmth.

Then I sang for a while. Music was conjured from me while I listened. Hymns without words floated on tunes I had never heard. They soaked into the silence that hung above the desert land, and I listened to this too.

My service completed itself with a prayer. It was a prayer of my own devising, conceived on my passage through the mountains. Indian youths climbed down from Cuchama with their vocation in life, and now I felt the power of my own. It was expressed within the words of this prayer.

"Lord and Mother, give me the power to do your work; the strength not to claim it as my own; and the freedom to enjoy it."

The sun prepared to douse itself in the Pacific Ocean. A bat fluttered up to catch insects ripe with altitude as the first of the stars appeared. Crickets turned electric and pulsed out sound. The lights of Tecate spangled. I dressed and began my descent.

Poor Tecate. Its display of lights grew more vulgar as I got lower, orange street lamps flushing like imitation orbs of gold. I looked back to the mountaintop and felt it pulling gently at the sides of my head. The night was warm and I knew I had this sacred mountain all to myself. I took off my clothes to stand naked, then turned and climbed it once again.

The city of San Diego over to the East was visible now. It spread its sheets of street lighting between dips in mountain ridges like wide phosphorescent bays in the Pacific. Hills ranged as silhouettes in different degrees of darkness. Aeroplanes at the same height as me tracked their twin beams of light to float passengers about the sky. Tecate still looked vulgar with its brash lights, but I felt more kindly toward it. To one side of the weather station, beyond its barbed wire fencing, was a broad flat rock still filled with warmth from the Sun. I took off my glasses and lay back to stretch across it.

Then I reached to put my glasses back on. I needed to check the sight above me. I had never seen so far beyond our regular stars. The lights of the constellations, the dusting of the Milky Way, were like the usherette's flashlight that shows you to your place before the film show begins. Massed behind these stars, and ranged beyond those, were stars that dimmed their brightness to the smallest flecks of dust so they could fit beside others on the screen of my view, shading the most distant darkness with the faintest sheen of light.

I sat up and prayed and wondered again, while the wind buffed my sides.

~~~~~~~~~

I drove up through the California Coastal Ranges. James hurried down the mountain path to greet me as I arrived. After the silence of his Zen retreat words didn't come easily. Mostly he smiled and he laughed. He lifted wide the black flaps of his robe, and we hugged.

I had the honour of attending the closing ceremony of this retreat. A chosen monk had reflected upon a koan, a simple statement of Zen truth, for ninety days. This ceremony in the zendo, the centre's beautiful wooden meditation hall, took the form of dharma combat. He elucidated the meaning of the koan, while other monks threw questions that challenged his understanding.

After such an intense period of silence and self-discipline as their long retreat, the occasion took on some lightness of spirit for the participants. Laughter bubbled through the wisdom, a laughter that came from relief rather than sudden insight. On a personal level, I recognized that the ceremony also marked a closing stage in my own spiritual journey. The ceremony moved me deeply.

The abbot of the monastery, Taizan Maezumi Roshi, presided from his chair with immense dignity. Afterwards James led me forward to meet him.

Maezumi had shown an interest in James's romantic attachments over the years. He had studied a picture of a naked man, trying to discover the gay aesthetic and giggling when he achieved it. He had listened to stories of those young men who James hoped to become involved with, and at these stories he had either snorted, or laughed. About myself, he was different. He had asked questions, and
~~~~~~~~~

remembered earlier references James could not remember himself. And he made an immediate and wonderfully Japanese request.

"We must have a photograph together!"

So this was how we met, the three of us clambering up the boulders of a rock garden to pose for our photograph. He had been a spiritual father for James. He was to die on a visit to Japan before a year had passed. It is good to have this photograph as a memory of him, the sun gleaming from his head, so short a man yet so erect and balanced and perfect on his rock.

We parted. It was later, as we were squeezing past each other along a wooden walkway, that a woman put us together and left us standing. "You have something to say to each other," she insisted.

I thanked Maezumi for allowing me to attend the dharma combat, and told him that the occasion was very beautiful.

"Ha!" he snorted, and waved his hand to dismiss the whole thing. "Too friendly!"

I roared with laughter. He looked at me, smiled, then laughed too.

"Too friendly!" he repeated, enjoying his own joke.

I thanked him for the teachings he had given to James. I loved James's tales of the earnest efforts he had laid at Maezumi's feet. I termed Maezumi's responses 'puncturing wisdom'. Rather than congratulate anyone on steps they had made along the spiritual path, he preferred to point out how hazardous the following steps would surely be.

"I am not James's teacher," he now told me. He waved a hand to indicate the surrounding trees, the mountains and the sky. "Nature. Nature is his teacher."

He invited me back to the Mountain Centre whenever James returned. I must spend days exploring the mountain tops, he told me. He had loved doing so himself. The mountain range stretched from there to the Pacific Ocean.

"What do you feel about mountains?" I asked him. "Do you think they are individual beings? Can we communicate with them?"

"Of course," he said. He turned and tipped back his head to look up at those mountains above us, then turned to face me.

"That is my name. Taizan Maezumi," he reminded me. "Taizan means Big Mountain."

Postscript
Guadalupe Peak

Bright stars and a slither of moon were clear through the end panel of the tent, set high up on the mountain's side. Sleep held me through the night, though many times I broke the surface into consciousness. A long dream persisted, writing chapter after chapter of itself, setting a message in place for the years to come.

It was still dark as I climbed from the tent. Starlight faded as I walked up the last stretch of mountain path. I sat on the rock where I had sat for my revelation of a year before and waited for the sun to rise across to my left. It began by colouring the clouds above it with a shine like a seascape, and washed pink light between the Douglas Firs on the mountaintop below. This mountaintop sloped at a steep angle to receive the light of dawn.

The scene before me was grand and pleasant, but the sense of revelation from a year before had faded. I waited till the sun was high enough to touch me with its heat, stood and climbed a little further, then prepared to go home.

This was the first mountain I ever heard speak. However no special words came from it this time. I paused to say a final goodbye. My hopes for this visit were always unclear, and now they were nothing but a shimmer of sadness. There was life on a spiritual plain, which had touched me with rapture then faded again. And there was my life on Earth, to which I was resigned.

The mountaintop responded to my farewell. It offered me no words, no shockwaves, but something gentle and complete. The mountain radiated me its love. It touched me as a warmth to the head first of all, then through my head down to my whole body.

I spoke to the mountain, thanked it and prayed to it. The mountain's love came back to me in pulses, as a conversation rather than a constant flow. I said goodbye and climbed down from my view of this mountaintop -- and now the words came. They were placed in my head rather than in my heart.

"You think love's a gift," the chiding began, "but it's a state of being. We mountains showed you where to work at love, but you stopped.

"Where's James now, the one we brought you to love? Alone at home. The love between you and James seemed to die this last week, didn't it? It snapped off as a sexual force, and you haven't known what to do about it. Do you know why this happened? You were using your love as a distraction. The love between you is important, very important, but it exists to serve all of life. That is its purpose. That's the purpose of love.

"You're waiting for death to rescue you from life, and don't care enough for the life you have. You're learning nothing. You're more intent on your own spiritual journey than on James's. That cannot be. It's not the way of love. James has his own rich life he needs to fulfill. It's hard, it's tough, and he needs your help. So do it. Help those you love to be better than yourself. Then let them help you. Get living, Martin. Get living."

And I recalled the messages from my dream of hours earlier. It had assured me that if both James and I worked and worked we would write something that was worthwhile; that celebrity and the social whirl were a distraction; and that the frank admission of our sexuality was vital.

I have worked and worked. I hope the mountains whispered as these pages turned.

Endnote

This book was helped by the award of a writer's bursary from the Scottish Arts Council, and an award from the K. Blundell Trust, administered by the Society of Authors.

The visits to Mount Ararat, Croagh Patrick, Arunachala, St Thomas Mount and Adam's Peak, as recorded in this book, took place between June and December 1993. The time in Germany was from 1991–92. The events in the chapters on Birling Gap, Guadalupe Peak, Chaco Canyon, the Sierra Nevada, Cuchama, and the meeting with Taizan Maezumi Roshi happened in 1994. The visit to Tirupati was in the spring of 1995, and the postscript on Guadalupe Peak was from the autumn of that year. The book was started in Birling Gap, continued in my homes in the mountains of New Mexico and the French Pyrenees, and finished in Sandy, Bedfordshire during January 2002.

My journeys around the world's mountains brought me into contact with many people. They have helped shape this story and my life. I thank them for their guidance and companionship.